Palgrave Studies in Sound

Series Editor
Mark Grimshaw-Aagaard
Musik
Aalborg University
Aalborg, Denmark

Palgrave Studies in Sound is an interdisciplinary series devoted to the topic of sound with each volume framing and focusing on sound as it is conceptualized in a specific context or field. In its broad reach, Studies in Sound aims to illuminate not only the diversity and complexity of our understanding and experience of sound but also the myriad ways in which sound is conceptualized and utilized in diverse domains. The series is edited by Mark Grimshaw-Aagaard, The Obel Professor of Music at Aalborg University, and is curated by members of the university's Music and Sound Knowledge Group.

Editorial Board:
Mark Grimshaw-Aagaard (series editor)
Martin Knakkergaard
Mads Walther-Hansen
Editorial Committee:
Michael Bull
Barry Truax
Trevor Cox
Karen Collins

Anders Eskildsen

Soundpainting

Collaborative Creativity in Conducted
Improvisation

Anders Eskildsen
Department of Communication and Psychology
Aalborg University
Aalborg, Denmark

ISSN 2633-5875　　　　　　　ISSN 2633-5883　(electronic)
Palgrave Studies in Sound
ISBN 978-981-96-1689-3　　　ISBN 978-981-96-1690-9　(eBook)
https://doi.org/10.1007/978-981-96-1690-9

© The Editor(s) (if applicable) and The Author(s), under exclusive license to Springer Nature Singapore Pte Ltd. 2024
This work is subject to copyright. All rights are solely and exclusively licensed by the Publisher, whether the whole or part of the material is concerned, specifically the rights of translation, reprinting, reuse of illustrations, recitation, broadcasting, reproduction on microfilms or in any other physical way, and transmission or information storage and retrieval, electronic adaptation, computer software, or by similar or dissimilar methodology now known or hereafter developed.
The use of general descriptive names, registered names, trademarks, service marks, etc. in this publication does not imply, even in the absence of a specific statement, that such names are exempt from the relevant protective laws and regulations and therefore free for general use.
The publisher, the authors and the editors are safe to assume that the advice and information in this book are believed to be true and accurate at the date of publication. Neither the publisher nor the authors or the editors give a warranty, expressed or implied, with respect to the material contained herein or for any errors or omissions that may have been made. The publisher remains neutral with regard to jurisdictional claims in published maps and institutional affiliations.

Cover illustration: Pattern © Melisa Hasan

This Palgrave Macmillan imprint is published by the registered company Springer Nature Singapore Pte Ltd.
The registered company address is: 152 Beach Road, #21-01/04 Gateway East, Singapore 189721, Singapore

If disposing of this product, please recycle the paper.

For Signe and Johanne

Contents

1 **A Sign Language for Conducted Improvisation**   1
  Gestural Communication and Conducted Improvisation   4
  The Emergence of Soundpainting   8
  Soundpainting Research and Community Publications   11
  Ground Rules   13
  "Live composing" or "conducted improvisation"?   14
  About This Book   16
  References   17

2 **Language Structure: Foundations of Meta-agentic Communication**   23
  The Meaning of Syntax   24
  The Syntax: Who, What, How, When   26
  Exceptions, Inconsistencies, and Finiteness   28
  A Rigid Communication Protocol for Open-Ended Instruction   30
  References   32

3 **What to Do and How to Do It: Fostering Creativity with Constraints**   33
  Indicating Openness   35
    Brainstorming and Immediacy with [Scanning] and [Point to Point]   36
    The Special Case of [Improvise]   39
  Indicating Specific Musical Content   41

	Combining Openness and Constraint	45
	Nuanced Constraint Using [With]	45
	References	49
4	**Cocreation: Distributing Agency in Interaction**	**51**
	The Social Nature of Authorship in Soundpainting	51
	Static Distributions of Agency	55
	The Soundpainter	55
	The Ensemble	59
	Dynamic Distributions of Agency	63
	Intra-ensemble Relations	63
	Content Developed Through Interaction	65
	References	69
5	**Change, Freeze, Develop: Organization and Transformation**	**71**
	Connecting Actions	73
	Past, Present, and Future	74
	Transformations	77
	Outcomes: Composition, Improvisation, and Beyond	81
	Broader Perspectives	82
	References	83

CHAPTER 1

A Sign Language for Conducted Improvisation

Imagine the beginning of a Soundpainting session, where you are in the role of "the soundpainter." You are responsible for conducting and guiding an ensemble, which in this case happens to be a group of musicians, through a collectively improvised performance. The experience could be described like this:

> You are standing in front of a group of musicians. They are positioned in a semicircle around you, and you have their full attention. With a few hand signs, you give the group a task: They should quickly prepare to come up with some simple, musical sounds. Using your arm as an imaginary spot highlighter, you scan the group. As your arm crosses each musician, they begin to play, stopping when the scanning arm has passed them by. As your arm sweeps across the group, you listen to each of the sonic contributions. The musicians present an eclectic mix of musical ideas. The bass player's simple and groovy ostinato seems like a solid foundation to build upon, so with a simple gesture, you sign the bass player to continue playing. You wait for a bit, letting the group listen and attune to the sounds of the bass. Then you sign the percussionist and a keyboard player to play something related to the bass player's contribution, and they improvise a groove. Now, the group has a musical foundation to build upon, and using another few signs, you tell the group to remember this particular musical setting, so they can find their way back to it later. You sign the guitar player to improvise a solo, and they begin building up ideas and phrases. After a bit, you sense a need to support the solo, so you sign the string and woodwind players to play

© The Author(s), under exclusive license to Springer Nature
Singapore Pte Ltd. 2024
A. Eskildsen, *Soundpainting*, Palgrave Studies in Sound,
https://doi.org/10.1007/978-981-96-1690-9_1

some background sounds using sustained notes with long durations. Soon, chord-like structures emerge, shifting and transitory, providing a dynamic background for the building solo. You sign the rest of the rhythm section to develop their current ideas, letting the groove evolve alongside the rest of the music. After a climactic section in the solo, you ask the musicians to turn back to the initial setting from before the solo. From here, many directions are possible, as you continue to guide and curate the improvised interactions between participants.

Participating in Soundpainting can be riveting, whether as a member of the musical ensemble, as the conductor (who is known as the soundpainter), or perhaps as a beholder of the performance. We are led on an unpredictable journey where the creative contributions of ensemble members feed into the musical result.

In Soundpainting, groups can collectively invent rich and unique musical soundscapes that none of the participants could ever have composed on their own. This can be done relatively easily, in a matter of mere seconds. Once a musical idea has been established, further work can then iterate on that to create larger pieces with dramatical developments and musical storylines.

Soundpainting is practiced in artistic and educational settings around the world, primarily with a focus on music, but also increasingly with an interdisciplinary focus on other forms of art. For the purpose of ensuring a certain level of proficiency and consistency as Soundpainting is being introduced in school systems around the world (Thompson, 2010, p. 77), a certification system offering multiple tiers of certification has been established, governed by Thompson and his closest collaborators. For budding soundpainters, several written tutorials are available for consultation alongside various online materials (further details can be found in the following sections), and training courses are conducted regularly by Thompson and other soundpainters.

At first sight, Soundpainting is quite demanding and, in a certain sense, restrictive. Participation requires attention, focus, and commitment from participants. It is also demanding in the sense that participants who are new to the practice are learning a new language with a specific and bounded set of communicational possibilities. This entails grasping a somewhat rigid set of syntactical rules, acquiring a vocabulary of strange hand movements, and understanding the instructions to which the gestures refer. Achieving fluency as a soundpainter, i.e., being able to execute strings of gestures clearly and understandably, requires further time and practice.

Getting started with Soundpainting as a member of the ensemble, however, is quite easy; when working with a competent soundpainter, understanding a few hand signs is enough to participate meaningfully in a Soundpainting performance. Delving deeper into the practice, the increased demands placed upon participants will be rewarded with rich interactions and surprising and creative musical outcomes.

When compared directly to freer forms of improvisation, Soundpainting appears to be a relatively restrictive system, given that participants in Soundpainting sessions are not free to do as they wish, and their room for maneuvering is constantly constrained by the soundpainter's instructions. And yet, musicians and other artists invest significant amounts of time and energy in learning, practicing, and disseminating Soundpainting. From my fieldwork as an ethnomusicologist and my own experiences as a soundpainter, it has become increasingly clear that the most important motivation behind the commitment to and practice of Soundpainting is this: Soundpainting can facilitate artistically rich interactions where creative agency arises through competent and rewarding interplay between participants. At its best, this can be an affective and exhilarating experience, which can lead to creative outcomes that one would never have been able to come up with otherwise.

This book delves into the workings of Soundpainting, analyzing the features of the sign language which in practice enable these creative, interactive processes. The individual chapters zoom in on key features and techniques. However, each chapter also places the practical insights from Soundpainting into a broader perspective, drawing upon theoretical knowledge about communication, creativity, interaction, and cognition. In doing so, I wish to discuss the interactive constitution of creative agency, which should provide crucial insight well beyond the circles of experimental and improvised music with which Soundpainting is usually associated. In other words, if we understand what is special about the rich and creative interactions that arise from Soundpainting, we might learn to harness the unending possibilities inherent in other improvised interactions. We might learn to craft practices in which humans collaborate to create performances in dialogical and interactive ways.

From research in the humanities and social sciences, we also know that what individuals can achieve always depends upon their environment and society. "No [hu]man is an island," as the English poet John Donne so eloquently expressed the social nature of human existence four centuries ago (Donne, 1624/1959, p. 108). As the current environmental crises make excruciatingly clear, our actions always take place in deep contexts, affecting our environment and others, including generations to come. We act in social settings and should be collectively accountable for our actions. And with its insistence on social interaction as a source of and site for creative agency, Soundpainting may inspire us to collectively navigate the uncertain terrains of an increasingly fractured social world.

This may sound like a boisterous claim, but my own experience in the Soundpainting community may serve as an initial explanation. In the spring of 2016, I visited Paris, an important site for Soundpainting due to its robust community of practitioners, to participate in a masterclass and certification session conducted by Walter Thompson and fellow soundpainter François Jeanneau. With participants from many different places and with diverse personal and professional backgrounds, the spoken languages were truly diverse. With several participants, I would have had difficulty conducting more than just a superficial conversation at the coffee machine due to a lack of linguistic common ground. But as the Soundpainting masterclass progressed over a couple of days, we were able to collaboratively create remarkably interesting and creative performances using relatively little ordinary discourse. This was a transformative moment for me, as it showed me how this unique and deceptively simple sign language could facilitate rich interaction processes among people who would otherwise not be able to coordinate and communicate effectively about a complex and uncertain collective process of improvisation. This confirmed my hunch that Soundpainting deserved further research and indirectly led to the writing of this book.

Gestural Communication and Conducted Improvisation

In order to understand how and why Soundpainting "works," it is useful to briefly revisit gestural communication and its and history in the context of musical performance. Early linguistic theories of language tended to disregarded nonverbal communication (Bavelas & Chovil, 2006, p. 98), but the use of nonverbal behavior in face-to-face dialogue has later become an important subject of study. We now know that gestures do not merely accompany speech but are often responsible for conveying or enhancing meaning in symbolic and nonredundant ways; "there is a growing body of […] evidence that the participants in a dialogue use gestures to communicate with each other" (Bavelas & Chovil, 2006, p. 110).

We also know that humans have the ability to attach symbolic meaning to gestures since this ability underpins what linguists refer to as natural sign language. Natural sign language emerges under certain social conditions, such as in families who raise deaf children; even if no family members learn any of the formalized systems for sign language, the use of gestures for communication emerges on its own (Engberg-Pedersen, 1998).

In the context of music, cognitive musicologists have suggested that "musical gestures" are at the heart of how humans experience music when performing and listening: "Music is basically a combination of sound and movement, and […] music means something to us because of this combination" (Godøy & Leman, 2010, p. ix). More specifically, a wide range of practices, from the shaman of quasi-religious rituals to the Western orchestral conductor, place an emphasis on hand/arm gestures; in these widely known practices, a central figure conducts or shepherds a group of performers in musical performance using hand gestures (Cottrell, 2007). In Western symphonic music, for instance, the conductor plays a key role in interpreting scores and bringing works of music to life.

If we understand a conductor's gestures as a medium of real-time communication, it is unsurprising that those who conduct large orchestras tend to employ hand gestures; if one wishes to communicate about an ongoing musical performance in real time, using a form of writing is simply too slow and impractical (technological media for written communication notwithstanding). Oral communication may also be difficult or even undesired in contexts where the sound of one's voice might disturb the sound of the ongoing performance. In contrast, the conductor's gestures can intuitively and precisely convey musical dynamics and timing.

What do we mean when we talk about communication in traditional practices of conducting in Western art music? A conductor's gestures are usually understood by the ensemble without explanation, as they relate to the gestures musicians make when playing their instruments. For example, larger and faster movements mean louder and more dramatic music. In these cases, communication between conductor and ensemble relies upon intuitive mappings of the conductor's gestures to features of the ensemble's musical performance. In terms of Peirce's well-known sign typology (Peirce, 1974), the conductor's gestures are indexical or iconic signs, i.e., they show the exact timing of musical action here and now, or they express musical dynamics by the similarity of gestural magnitude.

In Western art music, the general purpose of conducting is to temporally coordinate ensemble interpretation of music which has already been written. Since the Renaissance, standardized systems of musical notation have given us the ability to describe certain aspects of musical structure in writing. In the tradition of Western art music, written instructions, or scores, have been a very effective way of organizing music, as they provide a script for the performers to follow and interpret. This is especially relevant for large music ensembles, such as orchestras, where coordination and communication among many musicians are essential for creating meaningful and enjoyable musical experiences. Sometimes, a conductor is also present to help guide and shape the musical interpretation of the score. The creative work of composing the music is thus often separated into a process which precedes the presentation of the work in actual performance. For philosopher Lydia Goehr, this practice is a historical result of the cultural process in which the notion of the work of art became a deep-seated, ideological concept in Western art music culture (Goehr, 1994).

With the artistic revitalization of improvised music under terms like free jazz and free improvisation in the second half of the twentieth century (Lewis, 1996), however, the strict distinction between composer, performer, and conductor was renegotiated, as the improviser tends to integrate all these roles. In this "culture of spontaneity" (Belgrad, 1998), gestural communication began to be utilized in new and more complex ways.

Following the musical revolutions of bebop and free jazz in the mid-twentieth century, musicians and composers of improvised and experimental music began to develop frameworks for collective improvisation and live composition. These practitioners explored strategies and approaches to creating and arranging music "in the course of performance," as the improvisation scholar and ethnomusicologist Bruno Nettl once put it (Nettl, 1998). Many of these musicians experimented with gestural communication, and these experiments eventually led some artists to create quite elaborate systems of hand gestures that afford semantically complex communication about ongoing musical performances. These systems and the musical practices with which they are associated have later been termed "conducted improvisation" (Marino & Santarcangelo, 2013, p. 2).

Aside from Soundpainting, notable examples of contemporary systems for conducted improvisation include Lawrence "Butch" Morris's "Conduction" system, which is similar to Soundpainting in many respects but based on a comparatively more condensed set of gestures, Adam Rudolph's "Go: Organic" concept which combines gestural communication, graphic notation, and unique metric and rhythmic textures, Christine Duncan's hand signals for vocal improvisation, John Zorn's use of hand signs in his "Game Pieces," the Rova Quartet's "Radar" gestures, hand signals used for "conducted improvisation" in the London Improvisers Orchestra, gestural communication in Mats Gustafsson's "Fire! Orchestra," and many others. The examples listed here occur in no particular order and do not constitute an exhaustive survey of contemporary or historical approaches to conducted improvisation. See Marino (2013) and Marino and Santarcangelo (2013) for an attempt at a historical overview and a categorical definition of conducted improvisation.

The communicative innovation of these pioneers of conducted improvisation is their addition of a symbolic layer of meaning to the gestural communication. This is not to say that the individual signs in Soundpainting and similar frameworks do not employ indexicality or iconicity when needed, but the expansion to include symbolism was and is a crucial aspect of conducted improvisation.

Symbolism, again in Peirce's sence of the word (Peirce, 1974), entails that the form of the sign does not relate directly to its meaning. The meaning of symbols must instead be learned, typically through social exchange. When we read the word "red" in a piece of black text on a white background, for instance, we do not see an iconic resemblance of the perceptual quality of redness, and the letters that make up the word do not indicate another part of the text that is colored red; we know what "red" means because we have inferred or been taught what other people mean when they say or write "red" (Burks, 1949, p. 673). In a similar way, many signs in conducted improvisation need to be explained to participants before they can be used properly. Such signs work as devices for communication mainly due to social convention. Since the individual units of communication in Soundpainting generally (but not exclusively) convey meaning in this symbolical way, this book uses the term "signs," where the conventional discourse uses "gestures." The way one physically performs the different signs (i.e., the gestures) is certainly significant in practice, but insofar as this book is concerned with these units of communication, their potential for meaning-making and organization in improvised interactions is the main focus.

Why would musicians add the complexity of symbolic signs to an artistic context (jazz, improvised, and experimental music), which was already rich in musical variety and nuance? One reason why such symbolism is appealing or beneficial for musicians and other performers is that it allows for the use of language-like features in the course of musical creation. This book shows how a sign language that enables flexible and expressive communication can also allow a rich variety of musical possibilities to emerge in the moment. Soundpainting is an example of such a sign language that can convey complex musical ideas and processes and invite real-time creative input from the performers as they follow the instructions.

THE EMERGENCE OF SOUNDPAINTING

Soundpainting was invented by composer and musician Walter Thompson with inspiration from various strands of twentieth-century improvised and experimental music and other arts. Reflecting upon the origins of Soundpainting during an interview with musicologist Marc Duby, Thompson points out a connection between jazz, free jazz, and Soundpainting, stating that the latter generally can be seen as "a direct lineage of jazz" (Thompson, quoted by Duby, 2006, pp. 6–2), inscribing Soundpainting in a broader historical narrative of jazz and the AACM in the mid-twentieth century:

> So improvisation has gone from Charlie Parker opening up to this other thing, Miles [Davis] opening up to this other thing, Ornette [Coleman] opening up to this other thing, and Anthony Braxton who was my teacher, and then it opened up with other people in all kinds of ways, people, you know, taking in [Iannis] Xenakis, taking in [Karlheinz] Stockhausen, the AACM took in all of that, and those were my influences, along with Charles Ives [...]. I kind of see this as a direct lineage from jazz, not what Wynton Marsalis is doing as a direct lineage, not at all, but this, this, I see myself as directly coming from Charlie Parker. (Thompson, quoted by Duby, 2006, pp. 6–3)

Eschewing association with what some writers have dubbed a "neoclassical" strand of jazz, centered around musician Wynton Marsalis at the turn of the twentieth century (Nicholson, 2005), Thompson associates his oeuvre with that of Charlie Parker, who has been recognized as a highly original and inventive artist whose improvisational skill has been subject to both academic scrutiny and art world canonization (Lewis, 1996; Martin, 2002; Owens, 1974), serving as an inspiration for later generations of jazz musicians. Thompson's background was not purely musical though; Thompson's father was a painter, and early on in the development of Soundpainting, Thompson was inspired by Jackson Pollock, Willem de Kooning, and other abstract expressionist artists (Thompson & Minors, 2015a, 3:48). With an outlook to the spontaneity of abstract expressionism in visual art (Duby, 2006, pp. 6–8) and practices of improvised dance (Thompson, 2006, p. 12), Thompson's oeuvre has had a multidisciplinary scope from the outset.

As a highly formative educational experience, Thompson emphasizes five years of study in the 1970s with AACM member Anthony Braxton, an important figure within the creative music scene who also had experimented with gestural communication. Thompson states in *Workbook 1* that those years of study were "the most important of [my] life" (Thompson, 2006, p. 12). While studying with Braxton and attending the Creative Music School (a music school founded by Karl Berger, Don Cherry, and Ornette Coleman) in the 1970s, Thompson formed his first orchestra: "The focus of the orchestra was on large-group jazz-based improvisation. It was during these early days that Thompson began experimenting sith signing improvisation" (Thompson, 2006, p. 12).

According to Thompson's own account, the first sign in what would later become Soundpainting was invented in the middle of a performance in 1974; Thompson, directing the improvising orchestra, wanted to create a sonic texture of sustained notes underneath an improvising soloist and decided to sign what is now referred to as [Long Tone], thereby indirectly steering the soloist and the whole orchestra in a particular, aesthetic direction as the orchestra responded to the simple gestures (Thompson & Minors, 2015c, 0:50).

Following this early, improvised invention of gestures, Thompson began to invent other signs, and over the years, a more elaborate system for their use emerged. In this process, Thompson was heavily inspired by experimental composer Earle Brown's system for conducting his open-form compositions (Andersen, 2020), as well as the use of gestural communication in the course of performances by renowned jazz orchestra leaders Sun Ra and Duke Ellington's (Sabbe & Thompson, 2024, 13:52). Interestingly, Lawrence "Butch" Morris began to work on his system

Conduction in 1974 as well, and both creators moved to New York, where, according to Thompson, their parallel work served as mutual inspiration in what also amounted to a competitive, distanced relation (Thompson, 2014b). The two met in person several decades later to "bury the hatchet" and become "very close" (ibid.).

An important context for Thompson's early development of Soundpainting was a new orchestra formed in 1984, *The Walter Thompson Big Band*, which later became *The Walter Thompson Orchestra* (Thompson, 2006, p. 12). Initially, the idea behind using hand signs in this setting was to embellish the big band performance, adding improvised elements and sections during concerts. As Thompson and the orchestra continued working with the signs, a vocabulary of signs with rules for their use began to take form, eventually turning into what is now referred to as Soundpainting. Soundpainter and experimental composer Sarah Weaver explained to me that during this time, Soundpainting went from being used to fill in improvised sections or to add live embellishments during the performance of preexisting compositions to being a full language which could generate complete performances from scratch (S. Weaver, personal communication, September 22, 2023).

Since the mid-1980s, the number of Soundpainting signs has grown substantially as new ideas have been developed and other artists have learned Soundpainting and contributed with signs of their own. Since its inception, the language has thus been co-developed by a growing community of practitioners. For instance, the concept of the Soundpainting "syntax," which will be discussed further in Chap. 2, was formalized in the late 1990s in collaboration between Thompson and Weaver (Minors, 2012b). The official canon of Soundpainting signs, which are discussed in this book, is mainly described in Thompson's workbooks. But soundpainters around the world can and do invent their own signs, and additions to the canonized language are discussed and curated by a group of expert soundpainters in annual Soundpainting Think Tank events. According to Thompson's official web page, there are more than 1500 signs in the Soundpainting language (*Soundpainting | Soundpainting*, n.d.). Having been in development for several years (W. Thompson, personal communication, September 8, 2024), the long-awaited *Soundpainting Dictionary* was published in late 2024 (Thompson, n.d.). The dictionary essentially serves as a glossary which lists and defines the meaning of all Soundpainting signs recognized by Thompson and the core Soundpainting community.

With the sustained efforts of Thompson and others in developing, documenting, and teaching Soundpainting in different parts of the world, Soundpainting constitutes one of the most widely known and practiced forms of conducted improvisation. A central Soundpainting community website features information about ensembles in different countries as well as calendars for workshops and performance events (SOUNDPAINTING. ORG, n.d.). In terms of dissemination, Soundpainting is paralleled only by Conduction (Butch Morris's system), which, thanks to an important effort by a team of editors, recently has been documented in a book in much the same way that Thompson's workbooks document Soundpainting (Morris, 2017; Thompson, 2006, 2010, 2014a, 2022; Thompson & Harris, 2017).

While the size of the global Soundpainting community is difficult to ascertain, the largest active online forum for discussion of signs and announcements of Soundpainting events has around two thousand members (*Soundpainting Geeks | Facebook*, n.d.). The number of practitioners who participate in Soundpainting is likely significantly larger, since the majority of the active forum members appear to be ensemble leaders or teachers who teach or work with Soundpainting, as opposed to the much larger group of participants who participate in Soundpainting as ensemble members.

SOUNDPAINTING RESEARCH AND COMMUNITY PUBLICATIONS

With such a wide circle of practitioners, Soundpainting was bound to attract academic interest. It has thus been the subject of several research publications, including PhD dissertations, journal articles, and interviews. In broad terms, the main body of Soundpainting research has focused on the history, conceptualization, and practice of Soundpainting (Duby, 2006; Faria, 2016; Millà, 2021; Minors, 2012a, b, 2013, 2020; Waade, 2016). A strand of recent research focuses on the utility and effects of using Soundpainting in different contexts, from education at various levels (Coşkuner, 2016; Giacco & Coquillon, 2021; Vidal Belda, 2021) and psychometric tests of attention effects (Coşkuner & Stalheim, 2020) to adaptation of the system for therapeutic purposes (Espartero-Junquera, 2024). Another line of research focuses on computer recognition and the use of Soundpainting gestures in and beyond musical contexts (Couture et al., 2018; Dongo et al., 2019; Jáuregui et al., 2019a, b; Pellegrini et al., 2014; Van Nort, 2018).

Many other (i.e., nonresearch) publications have been produced on Soundpainting, including Thompson's instructional workbooks (Thompson, 2006, 2010, 2014a, 2022; Thompson & Harris, 2017) and a practical tutorial for music teachers with an emphasis on musical ensemble playing and improvisation (Duckert & Rasmussen, 2016). Thompson's own workbooks include accompanying video materials, most of which have been released online (Thompson, 2017d, e, h), demonstrating how to perform the gestures as defined in the workbooks and featuring performance examples in which the signs are used. Additionally, videos featuring explanations of the signs in *Workbook 1* in Spanish (José Carlos Ibañez, 2015) and French (TheMusicOfTheSilence, 2013) have been published.

Other online video materials about Soundpainting include a set of explanatory videos about Soundpainting's ground rules, how to perform the basic gestures, and the philosophy behind the sign language, published by Thompson (Thompson, 2017a, b, c, f, g), a set of introductory and practical videos by soundpainter Ceren Oran produced for the BIG BANG Festival in Ottawa in 2021 (Oran, 2021), as well as a demonstration video showcasing basic signs and responses by a multidisciplinary ensemble (i.e., featuring two musicians, an actor, and a dancer) produced by Oran, featuring Thompson as the soundpainter (Oran, 2017).

A four-part interview between Thompson and soundpainter/music researcher Helen Julia Minors offers a broad introduction to Thompson's work with Soundpainting, covering the historical context, definitions, and syntax of the language (Thompson & Minors, 2015a), multidisciplinary live composition (Thompson & Minors, 2015b), educational aspects of Thompson's oeuvre (Thompson & Minors, 2015c), as well as audience reception and broader affordances of Soundpainting (Thompson & Minors, 2015d).

Other interviews with Thompson (Kummrow, 2021; Pernas & Thompson, 2024) grant access to further community exchange, and numerous video-documented conversations between Thompson and soundpainter Johan Sabbe serve as an interesting archive of conversations about more advanced topics in the use and meaning of particular signs (Sabbe, n.d.). Finally, in addition to the sources mentioned here, online video platforms, primarily YouTube, contain a cornucopia of performance video recordings through which a wide variety of usage examples can be studied.

Ground Rules

To participate in Soundpainting, one must understand the fundamental conventions of the practice. As with any complex artistic practice, the "etiquette," as Howard Becker (2000) would put it is, in part, a tacit, embodied kind of knowledge that is best learned through practical participation. But many of the expectations that Soundpainting and similar forms of conducted improvisation rely upon have been defined, discussed, and formalized. This makes Soundpainting a rich object of study not only for artists and researchers who are interested in musical creativity but also for those who teach improvisation and creative performance practices; the conventions and expectations that aid the soundpainter in facilitating rich and creative interactions are well-defined and easy to understand. Thompson, for instance, lays out some key expectations for ensemble members in his *Workbook 1*:

- "When in doubt, don't lay out!" (Thompson, 2006, p. 8). In case an ensemble member is unsure whether to perform or not, commitment to action is preferred over passivity.
- "There are no mistakes!" (ibid.) In cases of misunderstandings or self-perceived errors, ensemble members should carry on and stand by the chosen course of action.
- "Don't sneak in, don't sneak out!" (ibid.) This means that ensemble members should begin playing only when so instructed by the soundpainter, and conversely one must continue to play until stopped explicitly by the soundpainter. When instructed to start or stop, ensemble members should do so precisely at the indicated point in time (or gradually, if that is part of the instruction).

Duckert and Rasmussen's *Ensemble playing and improvisation with Soundpainting* offers an additional ground rule:

- "Everything the soundpainter hasn't specified is up to the individual musician" (Duckert & Rasmussen, 2016, section 9). Ensemble members are encouraged to creatively interpret the instructions; if the soundpainter asks for a sustained note but does not specify the exact pitch, timbre, or loudness, the ensemble member is free to choose these parameters.

The implications of these rules and expectations will be discussed further in the remaining chapters of this book.

"Live composing" or "conducted improvisation"?

This book deviates from the "official" Soundpainting terminology in at least one obvious way: Whereas the general discourse around Soundpainting defines it as a "multidisciplinary live composing sign language" (Thompson, 2006, p. 5), this book describes Soundpainting as "conducted improvisation." Why deviate in this way?

Like related musical practices, Soundpainting does not lend itself to simple categorization as either composition or improvisation, as it incorporates aspects of both kinds of musical activity. In interviews, Thompson has explained that his personal understanding of the term "composition" is broad and not restricted to music (Thompson & Minors, 2015a, 10:28), related to the general idea of combining components into a greater whole: "Composition is structuring things" (Sabbe & Thompson, 2024, 9:35). In this perspective, improvisation is understood as "a form of composition" (Thompson & Minors, 2015a, 10:40), in the sense that improvising involves creating musical materials which, over the course of an improvised performance, combine and add up to a greater whole, a composition.

In an interview with Bruno Faria, "Thompson reflected upon soundpainting as a medium that allowed him to merge improvisation and composition, to keep *his feeling* as an improviser while he composed" (Faria, 2016, p. 98). This leads Faria to suggest that in Soundpainting, "the orality of improvised musical speech and the literacy of composed/performed musical writing/interpreting are brought together" (Faria, 2016, pp. 98–99). Butch Morris expressed similar ideas about Conduction, his system for conducted improvisation that bears many similarities to Soundpainting (Eskildsen, 2017), describing it as "giving rise to new forms of collectively motivated and organized musical expressions, allowing me to pursue the goal of constructing music in real time, within the intermediate space between notation and improvisation" (Morris, 2017, p. 35).

As Thompson's (and Morris's) considerations hint at, we should take care to avoid simplistic definitions of improvisation and composition as a binary pair of opposed or contradictory terms; stemming from the culture of Western art music in the late eighteenth century, the understanding of improvisation/composition as a simple dichotomy has been discussed at length in the field of improvisation studies (Brown, 2011; Feisst, 2016; Lewis & Piekut, 2016; Nettl, 1998) and generally been discarded as "ideologically driven [...] with clear prejudices in favor of the latter's presumed advantages of unity and coherence in musical utterance" (Lewis & Piekut, 2016, p. 3). This does not mean, however, that the widely used and quite useful concepts of improvisation and composition should be abandoned entirely; we must instead rethink the relationship between the two and situate our use of either term in relation to specific musical phenomena.

To clarify, then, how and why this book draws upon the concept of improvisation: In referring to Soundpainting as conducted improvisation, I do not deny that Soundpainting can be understood as a form of live or real-time composing, in the sense that a work of art is being composed and performed simultaneously. Nor do I wish to call into question whether the soundpainter can be understood as a composer, whose role in orchestrating and organizing the materials of the performance is crucial and qualitatively distinct from the role of the ensemble member. And finally, I do not suggest that we understand Soundpainting as "collective free improvisation" (Canonne, 2013, p. 40) or "pure" (ibid.) or "non-idiomatic improvisation" (Bailey, 1992, pp. xi–xii).

Rather, with the term "conducted improvisation," the present analysis highlights Soundpainting's potential to facilitate improvised interactions. Following Edgar Landgraf, a key theoretical thinker in improvisation studies, this entails understanding improvisation not as opposed to or distinct from composition, preparation, and premeditation: "Improvisation cannot be decoupled from structure and repetition; rather than being the expression of unbridled freedom, improvisation must be seen as a mode of engaging existing structures and constraints" (Landgraf, 2011, p. 11). In Soundpainting, "existing structures and constraints" include the sign language and the conventions for its use as well as the knowledge and practical capabilities of participants in each Soundpainting performance.

Furthermore, one might suspect that Soundpainting, with its elaborate sign taxonomy and system of "ground rules" and conventions, would somehow be contrary to improvisation, as improvisation is often (superficially) associated with the absence or avoidance of such preexisting materials and rules. As Judith Butler has argued on the topic of "rules," however, the relationship between improvisation and rules is not as straightforward as one might initially expect:

We wouldn't understand improvisation if there were no rules. In other words, improvisation has to either relax the rules, operate outside the rules, bend the rules – it exists in relation to rules, even if not in a conformist or obedient relation. (McMullen & Butler, 2016, p. 25)

Similarly, Landgraf has argued at length that "improvisation is not about the absence of rules and structures, […] but rather can be understood as a self-organizing process that relies on and stages the particular constraints that encourage the emergence of something new and inventive" (Landgraf, 2011, p. 5). In this sense, conceptualizing Soundpainting as improvisation invites us to study how processes based on Soundpainting are organized and staged, which means—among other things—studying how its "rules" and conventions promote the emergence of creative acts. This includes examining how the language's design and constraints afford co-creative interactions in which participants collaborate to create interesting and productive performances. Given the language's historical affinity with twentieth-century jazz and improvised music in North America, conceptualizing Soundpainting as improvisation entails discerning how Soundpainting embodies an "ethics of cocreation" (Fischlin et al., 2013) that characterizes these traditions.

About This Book

This book is not a how-to guide for learning how to sign the Soundpainting gestures, nor is it a catalog of Soundpainting signs—such materials exist already, as mentioned earlier. This book has emerged from my research into Soundpainting over the last decade, which includes fieldwork and interviews with key actors in the Soundpainting community. I am also a certified soundpainter and have taught Soundpainting workshops; so I have a firm knowledge of the language from a practitioner's perspective. This book details my analysis of how Soundpainting works, covering the reasons why this interesting practice—when facilitated with care and competence—can generate so rich interactions between participants. To support and extend this analysis, I draw upon theoretical knowledge from linguistics, sociology, musicology, systems theory, and more. The book is for anyone who wants to understand how and why Soundpainting works— both from a Soundpainting-internal perspective and from interdisciplinary research perspectives. Soundpainting can teach us much about creativity, interaction, and communication—in and beyond music and other arts. As an installment in the Palgrave Studies in Sound series, this book focuses on the use of Soundpainting in the context of sound and thus music, but it should be noted that Soundpainting has been extended to include an array of art forms beyond sound and music, including dance, theater, and visual art. For further information on Soundpainting in these settings, see Thompson (2017h, 2022) as well as Thompson and Minors (Thompson & Minors, 2015c).

When reading this book, you will be faced with this form of notation: [Whole Group][Minimalism][Play]. It is not a standard notation but merely constitutes a straightforward way to notate a succession of three distinct Soundpainting signs—in this case [Whole Group], [Minimalism], and [Play]. These specific signs will be discussed further in the following chapters.

The chapters can be read independently but are easier to understand if read sequentially since each chapter builds upon the preceding one. Chapter 2 introduces the Soundpainting syntax, i.e., how distinct kinds of signs may be combined, and discusses the broader function and meaning of this syntax. Chapter 3 discusses a wide range of signs that specify instructions for what ensemble members should do, ranging from open-ended content signs that invite ensemble members to improvise through signs that specify different kinds of musical content, to signs that combine these two categories, altogether constituting a nuanced taxonomy for specifying musical action in various degrees of specificity. Chapter 4 discusses the interactive basis of Soundpainting, including static and dynamic distributions of agency, and discusses the social nature of authorship in Soundpainting. Chapter 5 concludes by discussing how musical materials may be co-constructed, combined, and developed into coherent, temporally extended compositions.

REFERENCES

Andersen, D. (2020). (Per)forming Open Form: A Case Study with Earle Brown's Novara. *Music Theory Online, 26*(3). https://doi.org/10.30535/mto.26.3.1

Bailey, D. (1992). *Improvisation: Its Nature and Practice in Music*. The British Library National Sound Archive.

Bavelas, J. B., & Chovil, N. (2006). Nonverbal and Verbal Communication: Hand Gestures and Facial Displays as Part of Language Use in Face-to-face Dialogue. In *The SAGE Handbook of Nonverbal Communication* (pp. 97–115). Sage Publications, Inc. https://doi.org/10.4135/9781412976152.n6

Becker, H. S. (2000). The Etiquette of Improvisation. *Mind, Culture, and Activity*, 7(3), 171–176.
Belgrad, D. (1998). *The Culture of Spontaneity*. University of Chicago Press.
Brown, L. B. (2011). Improvisation. In T. Gracyk & A. Kania (Eds.), *The Routledge Companion to Philosophy and Music* (pp. 59–69). Routledge.
Burks, A. W. (1949). Icon, Index, and Symbol. *Philosophy and Phenomenological Research*, 9(4), 673–689. https://doi.org/10.2307/2103298
Canonne, C. (2013). Focal Points in Collective Free Improvisation. *Perspectives of New Music*, 51(1), 40–55.
Coşkuner, S. (2016). A New Approach In Music Education Improving Creativity: Soundpainting Creativity. *Participatory Educational Research*, 4(1) Article 1.
Coşkuner, S., & Stalheim, J. (2020). Effects of Soundpainting Training on Attention. *Journal of History Culture and Art Research*, 9(1) Article 1. https://doi.org/10.7596/taksad.v9i1.2307
Cottrell, S. (2007). Music, Time, and Dance in Orchestral Performance: The Conductor as Shaman. *Twentieth-Century Music*, 3(31), 73–96. https://doi.org/10.1017/S1478572207000333
Couture, N., Bottecchia, S., Chaumette, S., Cecconello, M., Rekalde, J., & Desainte-Catherine, M. (2018). Using the Soundpainting Language to Fly a Swarm of Drones. In J. Chen (Ed.), *Advances in Human Factors in Robots and Unmanned Systems* (pp. 39–51). Springer International Publishing. https://doi.org/10.1007/978-3-319-60384-1_5
Dongo, I., Jáuregui, D. A. G., & Couture, N. (2019). A Study on the Simultaneous Consideration of Two Modalities for the Recognition of SoundPainting Gestures. In *Proceedings of the 31st Conference on l'Interaction Homme-Machine* (pp. 1–12). https://doi.org/10.1145/3366550.3372259
Donne, J. (1959). *Devotions upon Emergent Occasions; Together with Death's Duel*. The University of Michigan Press. https://www.gutenberg.org/ebooks/23772/pg23772-images.html.utf8 (Original work published 1624)
Duby, M. (2006). *Soundpainting as a System for the Collaborative Creation of Music in Performance* (Issue October). University of Pretoria.
Duckert, K., & Rasmussen, G. (2016). *Ensemble Playing and Improvisation with Soundpainting* (J. Faurholt, Ed.; S. Palmer, Trans.). Edition Wilhelm Hansen.
Engberg-Pedersen, E. (1998). *Lærebog i tegnsprogs grammatik*. Center for Tegnsprog og Tegnstøttet Kommunikation - KC.
Eskildsen, A. (2017). "The Art of Conduction: A Conduction Workbook" and "Ensemble Playing and Improvisation with Soundpainting". *Critical Studies in Improvisation*, 12(1).
Espartero-Junquera, M. (2024). Adaptation of Soundpainting to Music Therapy for adults with intellectual disability. *Misostenido*, 4(6).
Faria, B. (2016). *Exercising Musicianship Anew Through Soundpainting: Speaking Music Through Sound Gestures*. Lund University.

Feisst, S. (2016). Negotiating Freedom and Control in Composition: Improvisation and Its Offshoots, 1950 to 1980. In G. Lewis & B. Piekut (Eds.), *The Oxford Handbook of Critical Improvisation Studies* (Vol. 2, pp. 206–229). Oxford University Press.

Fischlin, D., Heble, A., & Lipsitz, G. (2013). *The Fierce Urgency of Now: Improvisation, Rights, and the Ethics of Cocreation*. Duke University Press.

Giacco, G., & Coquillon, S. (2021). On the Process of Sound Creation: Some Models for Teaching Artistic Creation in Music Using a Soundpainting Project in a French Primary School. *Visions of Research in Music Education*, 28(1) https://digitalcommons.lib.uconn.edu/vrme/vol28/iss1/4

Godøy, R. I., & Leman, M. (Eds.). (2010). *Musical Gestures: Sound, Movement, and Meaning*. Routledge.

Goehr, L. (1994). *The Imaginary Museum of Musical Works: An Essay in the Philosophy of Music*. Oxford University Press. https://doi.org/10.1093/0198235410.001.0001

Ibañez, J. C. (Director). (2015, February 26). *Soundpainting Workbook 1 en Español* [Video]. YouTube. https://www.youtube.com/watch?v=wb9-DGfhN5s

Jáuregui, D. A. G., Dongo, I., & Couture, N. (2019a). Automatic Recognition of Soundpainting for the Generation of Electronic Music Sounds. In *Proceedings of the International Conference on New Interfaces for Musical Expression* (pp. 59–64).

Jáuregui, D. A. G., Dongo, I., & Couture, N. (2019b, June). Automatic Recognition of Soundpainting for the Generation of Electronic Music Sounds. In *NIME 2019 – The International Conference on New Interfaces for Musical Expression*. https://doi.org/10.5281/zenodo.3672866

Kummrow, S. (Director). (2021, September 10). *Walter Thompson and I talk all things Soundpainting* [Video]. YouTube. https://www.youtube.com/watch?v=JLPDWu69liM

Landgraf, E. (2011). *Improvisation as Art: Conceptual Challenges, Historical Perspectives*. Continuum Books.

Lewis, G. E. (1996). Improvised Music After 1950: Afrological and Eurological Perspectives. *Black Music Research Journal*, 16(1), 91–122.

Lewis, G. E., & Piekut, B. (2016). Introduction: On Critical Improvisation Studies. In G. E. Lewis & B. Piekut (Eds.), *The Oxford Handbook of Critical Improvisation Studies* (Vol. 1, pp. 1–37). Oxford University Press.

Marino, G. (2013). Musichaosmos. Intersoggettività, gioco e costruzione del senso nell'improvvisazione eterodiretta. In B. Terracciano & D. Mangano (Eds.), *Il senso delle soggettività. Ricerche semiotiche. Proceedings of the XL congress of AISS* (pp. 101–110).

Marino, G., & Santarcangelo, V. (2013). The Enaction of Conduction: Conducted Improvisation as Situated Cognition. In D. Glowinski, M. M. Marin, &

A. Camurri (Eds.), *Proceedings of the Sixth International Conference of Students of Systematic Musicology (SysMus13)* (pp. 1–6). Casa Paganini-InfoMus Research Centre, DIBRIS-University of Genoa, Italy.

Martin, P. J. (2002). Spontaneity and Organisation. In D. Horn & M. Cooke (Eds.), *The Cambridge Companion to Jazz* (pp. 133–152). Cambridge University Press.

McMullen, T., & Butler, J. (2016). Improvisation Within a Scene of Constraint: An Interview with Judith Butler. In G. Siddall & E. Waterman (Eds.), *Negotiated Moments: Improvisation, Sound, and Subjectivity* (pp. 21–33). Duke University Press.

Millà, A. (2021). Soundpainting Sign Language: Possibilities and Connections with Tactileology. *Philosophies, 6*, 69. https://doi.org/10.3390/philosophies 6030069

Minors, H. J. (2012a). Music and Movement in Dialogue: Exploring Gesture in Soundpainting. *Les Cahiers de La Société Québécoise de Recherche En Musique, 13*(1–2), 87–96. https://doi.org/10.7202/1012354ar

Minors, H. J. (2012b). Reassessing the Thinking Body in Soundpainting. *How Performance Thinks*, 142–148.

Minors, H. J. (2013). Soundpainting: The Use of Space in Creating Music-Dance Pieces. In M. Wyers & O. Glieca (Eds.), *Sound, Music and the Moving-Thinking Body* (pp. 27–34). Cambridge Scholars Publishing.

Minors, H. J. (2020). Soundpainting: A Tool for Collaborating During Performance. In M. Blain & H. J. Minors (Eds.), *Artistic Research in Performance Through Collaboration* (pp. 113–138). Springer International Publishing. https://doi.org/10.1007/978-3-030-38599-6_7

Morris, L. D. "Butch." (2017). *The Art of Conduction: A Conduction Workbook* (D. Veronesi, Ed.). Karma.

Nettl, B. (1998). Introduction: An Art Neglected in Scholarship. In B. Nettl & M. Russell (Eds.), *In the Course of Performance: Studies in the World of Musical Improvisation* (pp. 1–23). The University of Chicago Press.

Nicholson, S. (2005). *Is Jazz Dead? (Or Has It Moved to a New Address)*. Routledge.

Oran, C. (Director). (2017, May 19). *Basic Soundpainting Gestures with Walter Thompson* [Video]. YouTube. https://www.youtube.com/watch?v=LUTg6n9kTUQ

Oran, C. (2021). *BIG BANG! Soundpainting | Video Series*. National Arts Centre | Centre National Des Arts. https://nac-cna.ca/en/video/series/map-big-bang-soundpainting

Owens, T. (1974). *Charlie Parker: Techniques of Improvisation*. University of California.

Peirce, C. S. (with Hartshorne, C., Weiss, P., & Burks, A. W.). (1974). *Collected Papers of Charles Sanders Peirce* (New ed.). Belknap Press of Harvard University Press.

Pellegrini, T., Guyot, P., Angles, B., Mollaret, C., & Mangou, C. (2014). Towards Soundpainting Gesture Recognition. In *Proceedings of the 9th Audio Mostly: A Conference on Interaction with Sound* (pp. 1–6). https://doi.org/10.1145/2636879.2636899

Pernas, A., & Thompson, W. (Producers). (2024, March 16). *Walter Thompson: A Dive into Soundpainting* [Video]. YouTube. https://www.youtube.com/watch?v=elC37XEZMMA

Sabbe, J. (n.d.). *Johan Sabbe* [YouTube channel]. YouTube. Retrieved June 24, 2024, from https://www.youtube.com/channel/UCaQpm9OvZ-_HCL5B5kSJMsg

Sabbe, J., & Thompson, W. (Directors). (2024, July 17). *Walter Thompson Interview* [Video recording]. YouTube. https://www.youtube.com/watch?v=Bbuq936ZVrQ

Soundpainting | Soundpainting. (n.d.). Retrieved February 2, 2024, from http://www.soundpainting.com/soundpainting/

SOUNDPAINTING.ORG. (n.d.). SOUNDPAINTING.ORG. Retrieved February 3, 2025, from https://www.soundpainting.org

Soundpainting Geeks | Facebook. (n.d.). Retrieved February 5, 2024, from https://www.facebook.com/groups/4383252451

TheMusicOfTheSilence (Director). (2013, January 4). *SoundPainting Workbook 1 Les gestes de base* [Video]. YouTube. https://www.youtube.com/watch?v=RLrP4%2D%2Dl1DY

Thompson, W. (2006). *Soundpainting: The Art of Live Composition, Workbook 1.*

Thompson, W. (2010). *Soundpainting: The Art of Live Composition, Workbook 2.* Self-Published.

Thompson, W. (2014a). *Soundpainting: The Art of Live Composition, Workbook 3.*

Thompson, W. (2014b, March 1). *Soundpainting Geeks | Butch Morris Created Conduction (a Live Composing Sign Language) 1974 in California | Facebook* [Post]. Facebook. https://www.facebook.com/groups/4383252451/posts/10151912365362452/

Thompson, W. (Director). (2017a, January 17). *Soundpainting Lesson 2—Walter Thompson* [Video]. YouTube. https://www.youtube.com/watch?v=nJkAWKKcqU4

Thompson, W. (Director). (2017b, January 17). *Soundpainting Lesson 3—Walter Thompson* [Video]. YouTube. https://www.youtube.com/watch?v=jWWZEyZ1ahc

Thompson, W. (Director). (2017c, January 17). *Soundpainting Lesson 4—Walter Thompson* [Video]. YouTube. https://www.youtube.com/watch?v=_C3mONfgs0c

Thompson, W. (Director). (2017d, January 17). *Soundpainting Workbook 1—The Art of Live Composition by Walter Thompson* [Video]. YouTube. https://www.youtube.com/watch?v=hp_AxCgtD1M

Thompson, W. (Director). (2017e, January 17). *Soundpainting Workbook 2—The Art of Live Composition by Walter Thompson* [Video]. YouTube. https://www.youtube.com/watch?v=tKFjZEUbYdU

Thompson, W. (Director). (2017f, January 17). *Soundpainting—Lesson 1—Walter Thompson* [Video]. YouTube. https://www.youtube.com/watch?v=YJQf0MDsNaA

Thompson, W. (Director). (2017g, January 19). *Soundpainting Lesson 5—Walter Thompson* [Video]. YouTube. https://www.youtube.com/watch?v=UuA25cg6Z7c

Thompson, W. (Director). (2017h, January 19). *Soundpainting Workbook 3—For Theatre and Danse by Walter Thompson* [Video]. YouTube. https://www.youtube.com/watch?v=dd0FztQIr5w

Thompson, W. (2022). *Soundpainting: The Art of Live Composition, Workbook 4*.

Thompson, W. (n.d.). *Soundpainting Dictionary*. Soundpainting. Retrieved February 3, 2025, from https://dictionary.soundpainting.com/

Thompson, W., & Harris, M. (2017). *Soundpainting: A Language of Creativity for Music Educators*.

Thompson, W., & Minors, H. J. (Directors). (2015a, January 18). *Soundpainting Interview with Walter Thompson Part 1* [Video]. YouTube. https://www.youtube.com/watch?v=oRLRVumJfhg

Thompson, W., & Minors, H. J. (Directors). (2015b, January 18). *Soundpainting Interview with Walter Thompson Part 2* [Video]. YouTube. https://www.youtube.com/watch?v=_WpILl0h6fU

Thompson, W., & Minors, H. J. (Directors). (2015c, January 29). *Soundpainting Interview with Walter Thompson Part 3* [Video]. YouTube. https://www.youtube.com/watch?v=rzeuBP8BUxk

Thompson, W., & Minors, H. J. (Directors). (2015d, February 12). *Soundpainting Interview with Walter Thompson Part 4* [Video recording]. YouTube. https://www.youtube.com/watch?v=HWASsgNq1Rc

Van Nort, D. (2018). Conducting the in-Between: Improvisation and Intersubjective Engagement in Soundpainted Electro-acoustic Ensemble Performance. *Digital Creativity, 29*(1), 68–81. https://doi.org/10.1080/14626268.2018.1423997

Vidal Belda, O. (2021). *Componiendo con soundpainting en el aula de música. Un estudio de casos colectivo sobre creación sonora colaborativa* (p. 1). [http://purl.org/dc/dcmitype/Text, Universitat de València]. https://dialnet.unirioja.es/servlet/tesis?codigo=301655

Waade, R. A. (2016). *Tegnspråk i musikken: Soundpainting som improvisatorisk-kompositorisk verktøy*. Doctoral thesis, NTNU. https://ntnuopen.ntnu.no/ntnu-xmlui/handle/11250/2431001

CHAPTER 2

Language Structure: Foundations of Meta-agentic Communication

In contemporary Soundpainting practice, one of the very first things that newcomers learn is "the syntax," which governs the soundpainter's communication with the ensemble. These syntactical conventions are simple to understand but also afford potentially quite complex, open-ended communication about creative agency.

Soundpainting came into existence as a few signs that designated certain kinds of musical content (Thompson, 2006, p. 12). These signs could be used for communication with an ensemble in the course of performance to indicate different kinds of musical content that the conductor would ask ensemble members to improvise.

Thompson soon developed new signs and used them in different musical settings, and other artists began to use the language and participate in Thompson's work. From the late 1990s, Sarah Weaver, an experimental composer based in New York, studied with Thompson and was the first person besides Thompson to be fully trained as a soundpainter, eventually becoming an associated soundpainter and participating in the annual Think Tanks, where a growing community of soundpainters would discuss the development of the language (S. Weaver, personal communication, September 22, 2023).

As the Soundpainting vocabulary and the complexity of meaning that could be conveyed continued to grow, Weaver identified a need to formalize a structure for the language (ibid.). Thompson and Weaver collaboratively established a limited set of sign categories and some directions for the order of signs belonging to different categories—"the syntax." A trained musician and composer, Weaver also held a degree in music education and was thus aware of how Soundpainting would or could be taught. The didactic benefit of a formalized language structure is that it enables clear communication and shared knowledge about how (complex combinations of) signs should be understood and used. Establishing the syntax laid the groundwork for further formalization in Thompson's official workbooks and certification system, providing a theoretical backdrop and for the development of new signs. Seen from this perspective, the syntax is a crucial condition for the flourishing and broad intelligibility of the language.

Dissecting the categories of signs and the conventions for their use, this chapter argues that the Soundpainting syntax constitutes a rather limited communication protocol; but in its construction and semantic scaffolding of communication, it is designed to facilitate processes where creative agency can arise in a collaborative dialogue between soundpainter and ensemble.

THE MEANING OF SYNTAX

When we travel to a foreign country where we do not understand the language, we may be able to rehearse a collection of isolated words or phrases in order to be able to ask for directions or read the menu at a restaurant. But having deeply meaningful and cocreative conversations with the inhabitants will likely prove difficult. In other words, language acquisition is not merely a question of committing a vocabulary to memory; learning how to communicate is also a question of learning how to *combine* the different elements of a language in contextually meaningful ways.

When a soundpainter conducts an ensemble, they can choose from all the signs that the ensemble understands. As mentioned in Chap. 1, many hundreds of signs have been invented on a global scale, although only a few hundred signs are officially defined in the Soundpainting workbooks (Thompson, 2006, 2010, 2014, 2022). Combining signs at random is not a good strategy, however; the order and combination of signs matter, just like in ordinary language. Phrases like "the cat chased the dog" and "the dog chased the cat" refer to one animal chasing the other, with roles reversed. The word order contributes to the meaning of the sentence—or detracts from it; "chased the dog the cat" does not make sense.

In Soundpainting, two commonly known signs, [Long tone] and [You], can illustrate a similar point. Using [Long tone] (which indicates sustained sound) to identify a member of the ensemble is not logical. Instead, [You] (carried out by simply pointing to one or more specific ensemble members) meaningfully directs instructions at specific addressees. [You], on the other hand, is not relevant for indicating exactly *what* an addressee should do, for which [Long tone] would be more suitable. Adding a [Play] sign to indicate *when* the instruction should be carried out, we can thus logically say that [You][Long Tone][Play], where the identified addressee begins to play sustained sounds exactly when the [Play] sign is given.

I am suggesting here that Soundpainting, by means of its syntactical conventions, shares a common trait with ordinary language. Compared to natural language, Soundpainting is an artificial construct, i.e., a rational design, which is different from the emergent result of sociolinguistic evolution that constitutes everyday language. It is useful, however, to introduce a few insights from modern linguistics to assist our understanding of the meaning and utility of Soundpainting's syntax. According to construction grammar, "the basic form of a syntactic structure is a construction—a pairing of a complex grammatical structure with its meaning" (Croft, 2010, p. 463). Soundpainting's artificial syntax can be understood as a construction, and its structure and meaning will be discussed below. Proponents of cognitive grammar generally assert that "[l]exicon and grammar form a continuum consisting solely of assemblies of symbolic structures" (Langacker, 2010, p. 438). Symbolic structures are understood here as specific pairings of form and meaning.

Grammatical forms, in other words, are not abstract rules to be followed, but inherently meaningful aspects of language use. The sentence "X flibbles Y," while somewhat nonsensical in its avoidance of actual words from a "lexicon," will immediately be recognized by most English speakers as a "Noun Phrase"-"Verb"-"Noun Phrase" structure, in linguistic terms. And that structure carries an abstract meaning: X, some kind of actant, in some unknown way does something in relation to some other object or actant, Y. The sentence lacks semantic specificity, since we don't know who or what X and Y are or what "flibbling" refers to. But since we understand that X is somehow doing something in relation to Y means that the structure carries an abstract meaning of agentic schematicity.

The syntax in Soundpainting should be understood as a construction or symbolic structure in this sense - the syntax carries an abstract, schematic meaning. Before discussing that meaning further, however, let us look more closely at the structure of the syntax and how it functions to create phrases for instruction.

THE SYNTAX: WHO, WHAT, HOW, WHEN

The syntax is four-fold and should, in Thompson's words, be understood like this: "The gestures in Soundpainting first identify *Who* is going to perform, followed by *What* type of improvisation is going to be performed, *How* the improvisation will be performed, and *When* to begin performing" (Thompson, 2006, p. 4).

This definition highlights two crucial aspects of how communication with Soundpainting works: First, the syntax establishes a canonical *typology* of signs. Soundpainting signs generally belong to one of the four main categories—who, what, how, and when. Second, the syntax specifies the *order* in which signs of different types may be given to form a logical instruction; any given Soundpainting sign may qua its category only occupy certain slots in a syntactically correct phrase.

Who	Who-signs identify one or more addressees within the ensemble and are thus also referred to as "identifiers" (ibid.). The who-sign thus defines who the soundpainter intends to address with their particular instruction. Here are some examples of commonly used who-signs: – [Whole Group]: The whole ensemble – [You]: One or more ensemble members being pointed to by the soundpainter – [Groups]: Subgroups within the ensemble – [Vocalists], [Percussion], [Strings], etc.: Groups defined by conventional instrument categories

(continued)

(continued)

What	What-signs specify which kind of action that addressees should perform and are also referred to as "content gestures" (ibid.). There are too many what-signs to mention here, but a few notable examples include: – [Long Tone]: A sustained note – [Pointilism]: Rapidly performed, arrhythmic, staccato notes – [Laugh] and [Speak]: Laughing and speaking – [Memory]: Musical content memorized during the course of the performance – [Scanning]: Improvisation when "being scanned" – [Palette]: Precomposed and rehearsed content It is worth noting that in *Workbook 2* (Thompson, 2010, p. 18), Thompson further divides the what-signs into three subcategories: "content gestures" (which refer to specific kinds of musical content, like [Long Tone] or [Pointilism]), "modes" (which entail that the ensemble follows and interprets the soundpainter's gestures in real time, like [Scanning]), and "palettes" (which are prepared before the beginning of the Soundpainting process and signed with the [Palette] sign).
How	How-signs, also referred to by Thompson as "modifiers" (ibid.), allow the soundpainter to modify the action that is to be performed. Some of the most common how-signs include: – [Volume Fader]: How quiet or loud to play – [Legato] and [Staccato]: As defined in conventional music notation and theory – [Blinders]: Ignore other ensemble members
When	When-signs, also referred to as "go gestures" (ibid.), specify the timing of the action. In order to initiate the action that has been specified in the currently signed phrase, the soundpainter steps forward into an imaginary box placed immediately in front of them, signing the gesture associated with the when-sign. Examples include: – [Play]: Begin to play immediately – [Off]: Stop playing immediately – [Enter/Exit Slowly]: Begin to play or stop playing, respectively, within a span of 5 seconds

Let us imagine a simple Soundpainting performance where the soundpainter signs the following phrase: [Whole group][Long Tone][Volume Fader (Low)][Play]. This phrase breaks down to the following instructions:

– all ensemble members (who)
– should soon play or sing sustained notes (what)
– at a low volume (how)
– beginning as the soundpainter steps into the imaginary box and completes the phrase (when)

The ensemble thus begins to perform sustained notes as the [Play] sign is given. What happens next? Well, the general rule in Soundpainting is that ensemble members continue to perform as instructed until they are instructed to do something else. In this example, the ensemble will simply keep sustaining the notes that they started playing/singing. The soundpainter might now choose to sign the phrase [Whole Group][Off], which instructs all ensemble members to stop performing. It is important to realize that ensemble members must continue performing as instructed while the soundpainter signs the next phrase; only when the when-sign of the following phrase is given should ensemble members begin to act differently.

Exceptions, Inconsistencies, and Finiteness

The [Off] sign is an example of a common exception to the syntax in that a single sign constitutes both a what- and a when-sign, signaling both what addressees should do (in this case, they should simply stop) and when they should carry this instruction out (in this case, immediately, as the soundpainter steps into the box and signs the gesture).

In the practical use of Soundpainting, there are many such deviations from the syntax, including exceptions, omissions, and shortcuts. For instance, having signed [Whole Group][Long Tone][Play], the soundpainter may then sign [Whole Group][Volume Fader], in which case the when-sign is implicit in the soundpainter's movement in space; when using [Volume Fader] without a what-sign, the ensemble adjusts the volume of their playing, as the soundpainter steps into the imaginary box in front of them.

Interestingly, [Long Tone][Play] or [Whole Group][Long Tone] would be considered syntactically incorrect/incomplete phrases since they omit who- or when-signs. In some what-signs such as [Scanning], the when-sign is implicit but easily discernible based on the soundpainter's movements in physical space.

Furthermore, many signs, especially from the more advanced parts of the language (Thompson, 2010), do not fall easily into one category, conflating for instance the distinction between content (what-signs) and modification (how-signs). In Chap. 3, further examples of such "internal conventional rule-bending" (Faria, 2016, p. 99) will be mentioned.

Exceptions aside, the syntax establishes a combinatory logic that—given the many possible permutations of signs—yields many different semantic possibilities. Even if only the 42 signs described in *Workbook I* are used, there are many possible permutations, and the number of syntactically correct combinations of signs is significantly larger than the number of individual signs.

In an interview with Marc Duby, Thompson noted several of the gestures which do not follow the syntactical rules discussed above, mentioning that "in each case, I had to break the rules to achieve my goals" (Thompson, quoted by Duby, 2006, p. 6:38). For Duby, the presence of these internal inconsistencies points to "the futility of attempting to finalize Soundpainting as a system with a finite and self-consistent set of rules" (ibid.). This view emphasizes the practical use of spoken and written language (Saussurean "parole"), as opposed to syntactical rules, which can be abstracted from such use (Saussurean "langue"). This highlights the fact that Soundpainting is a living language that changes and develops gradually as different practitioners use it. For instance, Vocal Painting, a method for conducting choral improvisation developed by professor of choir directing Jim Daus Hjernøe, is based on Soundpainting but does not utilize the syntax (J. D. Hjernøe, personal communication, August 13, 2024).

Contrasting Duby's perspective, Bruno Fario favors an understanding of languages as "systems that afford many expressive possibilities, including instances of internal rule-bending, through their finiteness and self-consistency" (Faria, 2016, p. 99). The boundedness of Soundpainting as an intelligible yet generative system can indeed be construed as one of its strengths:

> Like any medium for expression, soundpainting has its limitations. To different extents it conditions how ideas are communicated as well as its users' way of being. That should not necessarily be understood as a weakness, but as something that points to its integrity. (Faria, 2016, p. 99)

As Faria points out, Thompson has successfully maintained a self-consistent and coherent practice in Soundpainting through decades in which the practice spread across continents and artistic communities. The dissemination of Soundpainting from the late 1990s and onward owes its success in part to the immediate intelligibility of the syntax, which has turned out to be an important bit of theoretical scaffolding for use when teaching Soundpainting (S. Weaver, personal communication, September 22, 2023). Understanding the meaning of any given sign is simply easier once we know which type of sign it is according to the implicit typology of the syntax. Even with exceptions and deviations, the syntax functions as a context in which signs are placed to frame and explicate their meaning.

A Rigid Communication Protocol for Open-Ended Instruction

The syntax, as I see it, practically functions as a simple protocol for instructional communication, i.e., for instructing others on how to act. As such, the syntax ensures that each Soundpainting phrase specifies certain fundamental aspects of a future action. The language structure thus produces instructions that distribute, condition, enable, and transform agency.

The first signs in any phrase (who-what-how) do not affect what the ensemble is doing while receiving the instructions—only as the soundpainter signs the when-sign will the instruction be carried out. This, of course, requires ensemble members to multitask, constructing an understanding of instructions for something they will do in the future while performing something else at the same time. The movement in physical space by the soundpainter is a key grammatical marker, which, in conjunction with the specific signs used, shows addressees exactly when they should perform the specified changes in musical behavior.

Motion in space is not a prototypical indicator of grammatical function in ordinary language use, but it is not unheard of—natural sign languages make extensive use of physical space for grammatical indication (Wilcox, 2010, p. 1116). The shift between the soundpainter's position in or out of the imaginary box provides a way for ensemble members to switch from understanding what is being signed to acting in response to the instructions.

The mandatory who-slot thus forces the soundpainter to address either the whole ensemble, different subgroups of ensemble members, or individuals within the ensemble. In this way, the syntax enables a dynamic distribution of agency within the ensemble. Distribution of agency in Soundpainting will be discussed further in Chap. 4. Choosing a what-sign forces the soundpainter to select from the different kinds of musical content that can be referenced in the Soundpainting language, ranging from specific content such as a single sustained note to more open improvisation where the addressee has complete freedom to perform as they see fit. What-signs may be omitted from a phrase, but only if a how-sign is used instead, and vice versa. How-signs specify certain qualities of the action to be performed. Multiple how-signs can be attached to a single phrase in order to constrain different aspects of the action to be taken. Conversely, how-signs can also be—and often are—omitted entirely, leaving the unspecified parameters to be determined by the addressee.

These examples illustrate how the syntax affects the constitution of agency in Soundpainting. The basic questions of who will be doing something and when they will be doing it are usually determined not by individual ensemble members but by the soundpainter's instructions. A few Soundpainting signs deviate from this fixed scheme, some of which will be discussed further below. But we may conclude for now that regarding agency in Soundpainting, the syntax forces the soundpainter to make distinctions and indications about the who and the when of future actions in each and every phrase they sign. Furthermore, the syntax forces the soundpainter to specify what will be done, how it will be done, or a combination of these aspects—even if both aspects can be specified in a minimal way, leaving most decisions to the addressee.

Compared to the grammatical constructions of natural languages, the Soundpainting syntax is an artificial design that perhaps can be compared to the syntax for a programming language or a digital communication protocol, where the computer only understands the source code that is written in the correct order and the grammatical rules are followed to the letter. In this sense, the syntax is rather limiting, as the soundpainter does not have access to all of their natural language, which would lend itself to more flexible instruction and description.

But the limiting nature of the syntax is actually its strength. Once participants are fluent in signing and understanding Soundpainting phrases, the syntax ensures that the aforementioned aspects of agency are always clarified for all participants—even if the instructions are open-ended and intentionally leave room for interpretation. This distinguishes Soundpainting from freer forms of improvisation in a significant way; in collective free improvisation, many cognitive resources are devoted to achieving or negotiating a shared understanding of these aspects of interaction (Canonne, 2013; Canonne & Aucouturier, 2013; Canonne & Garnier, 2012). In Soundpainting, knowledge about who will be performing, which types and qualities of action they will perform, and when they will begin (or stop), can be shared across the ensemble.

Having a collective understanding of the distribution and scaffolding of musical agency across the ensemble due to the soundpainter's signs frees up cognitive resources for other tasks. Ensemble members can thus focus on other aspects such as their creative contributions, which will be discussed in the next chapter.

References

Canonne, C. (2013). Focal Points in Collective Free Improvisation. *Perspectives of New Music*, *51*(1), 40–55.
Canonne, C., & Aucouturier, J.-J. (2013). Play Together, Think Alike: Shared Mental Models in Expert Music Improvisers. *Psychology of Music*, *44*(3), 544–558.
Canonne, C., & Garnier, N. B. (2012). Cognition and Segmentation in Collective Free Improvisation: An Exploratory Study. In E. Cambouropoulos, C. Tsougras, P. Mavromatis, & K. Pastiadis (Eds.), *Proceedings of the 12th International Conference on Music Perception and Cognition and the 8th Triennial Conference of the European Society for the Cognitive Sciences of Music* (pp. 197–204).
Croft, W. (2010). Construction Grammar. In D. Geeraerts & H. Cuyckens (Eds.), *The Oxford Handbook of Cognitive Linguistics* (p. 0). Oxford University Press. https://doi.org/10.1093/oxfordhb/9780199738632.013.0018
Duby, M. (2006). *Soundpainting as a System for the Collaborative Creation of Music in Performance*. University of Pretoria.
Faria, B. (2016). *Exercising Musicianship Anew Through Soundpainting: Speaking Music Through Sound Gestures*. Lund University.
Langacker, R. W. (2010). Cognitive Grammar. In D. Geeraerts & H. Cuyckens (Eds.), *The Oxford Handbook of Cognitive Linguistics* (p. 0). Oxford University Press. https://doi.org/10.1093/oxfordhb/9780199738632.013.0017
Thompson, W. (2006). *Soundpainting: The Art of Live Composition, Workbook 1*. Self-Published.
Thompson, W. (2010). *Soundpainting: The Art of Live Composition, Workbook 2*. Self-Published.
Thompson, W. (2014). *Soundpainting: The Art of Live Composition, Workbook 3*.
Thompson, W. (2022). *Soundpainting: The Art of Live Composition, Workbook 4*.
Wilcox, S. (2010). Signed Languages. In D. Geeraerts & H. Cuyckens (Eds.), *The Oxford Handbook of Cognitive Linguistics* (pp. 1113–1136). Oxford University Press. https://doi.org/10.1093/oxfordhb/9780199738632.013.0042

CHAPTER 3

What to Do and How to Do It: Fostering Creativity with Constraints

In a recent PhD dissertation, Oscar Vidal Belda studied the use of Soundpainting in primary and secondary education centers in Valencia. In these contexts, Vidal Belda concluded, Soundpainting "contributes to current methodological approaches as a creative teaching and learning experience in that it provides teachers with strategies or practices that encourage students to create original music related to the development of their creative thought" (Vidal Belda, 2021, p. 18). This research project suggests that Soundpainting allows students and teachers to cultivate creativity both individually and collectively.

What is it about Soundpainting that leads to such grand conclusions about its ability to foster creative musical practice and inspire creative thinking? An anecdote from my own fieldwork provides some insight into this question: During one of my own first forays into Soundpainting in 2014, I participated in a course taught by Ketil Duckert and Gustav Rasmussen in Copenhagen, Denmark. Initially, participating as the soundpainter and composing in real time with signs such as [Long Tone] (sustained tones), [Pointilism] (chaotic swarms of short, arrhythmic sounds, and [Minimalism] (simple, repeated motifs) captured my imagination as exciting and fresh ways to imagine musical content. But the main insight came a bit later during the course, as the instructors began to emphasize signs that were intentionally open to performer choice, such as [Scanning] (improvise when pointed to by the soundpainter's scanning arm) or

© The Author(s), under exclusive license to Springer Nature Singapore Pte Ltd. 2024
A. Eskildsen, *Soundpainting*, Palgrave Studies in Sound, https://doi.org/10.1007/978-981-96-1690-9_3

[Relate To] (play something that relates to something else that is going on). These signs allowed for surprising musical ideas and wonderfully weird soundscapes to emerge from the combinations of sounds produced by the participants.

As a singular composer, even with unlimited time at my disposal, I could not possibly have come up with these musical expressions. Neither could the other participants, for that matter. The sounds that emerged simply lay beyond what any single participant could have imagined or composed through musical notation beforehand. And that realization is a powerful one; under certain conditions, Soundpainting sessions can bring about creative outcomes that no one participant could have imagined beforehand.

It seemed, at the time, somewhat paradoxical to me that a rather limited vocabulary to describe musical content could lead to such unpredictable outcomes. And yet, the utility of constraints in creative processes is generally well known in and beyond the artistic realm. According to philosopher Jon Elster, artists willingly bind themselves with seemingly strict constraints since such bindings, paradoxically, can "enhance and stimulate the creative process" (Elster, 2000, p. 209). Similarly, theater scholar Erik Exe Christoffersen argues that art's creative processes thrive in formal, restrictive frames composed of ground rules that function as "obstructions" (Christoffersen, 2011, p. 135).

Distinct from financial, practical, or political constraints, the kinds of "creative" constraints that Elster and Christoffersen discuss are consciously imposed on artists, either by themselves or by artistic collaborators. It is important to note here that "not all constraints will do equally well," as Elster puts it (2000, p. 209). Establishing constraints that generate interesting and creative processes, in other words, is an important skill in creative and/or artistic work. With too many options, taking creative action becomes difficult or unlikely, and so the number of options must be reduced.

To study Soundpainting is, in a way, to study the art and craft of facilitating interactive, constraint-based creativity. This chapter highlights the constraints on performer agency that the soundpainter may impose in the course of performance by means of what- and how-signs, thereby introducing what design researchers have called "decisive constraints," which are characterized by "radical decision-making and creative turning points" (Biskjaer & Halskov, 2014, p. 28). These signs frame the selectivity of the ensemble's improvisational agency. When viewed as a repertoire of open-ended instructions for creative action, the pool of what-signs grants access to the nontrivial and multifaceted connection between constraint and systemic openness to creative agency.

While the musical content is somewhat unknown at the outset of a Soundpainting performance, ensemble members who are familiar with Soundpainting expect to be addressed using a subset of the sign language. Even if the performance is part of an introductory workshop in which ensemble members are learning the signs and general concept of Soundpainting, a teacher (who in the beginning usually takes the role of the soundpainter) will show gestures related to and explain the meaning of at least a few signs before actually using the language. In this way, the communication is limited to the hitherto introduced signs.

Beyond beginner workshops, a pool of signs to be used during a performance has usually been decided beforehand, either implicitly during rehearsals or by explicit agreement within a group. The 42 signs described in *Workbook I* (Thompson, 2006), which comprise the fundamental level of Soundpainting, may serve as an imaginary example; when a set of 42 acceptable signs from the soundpainter has been fixed through previous interactions in a group, the "interaction system" (Kieserling, 1999) has a limited set of communicative operations at its disposal.

In scaffolding the possibilities for meta-communication by fixing a subset of signs to be used in performance, one might think that Soundpainting is restrictive or limiting. Only 24 of the 42 signs in *Workbook 1* are what-signs, and so it would appear that Soundpainting, at the fundamental level, only allows for 24 different types of musical content to be performed. But that is not the case; even a limited vocabulary of Soundpainting signs can open interactions up to the emergence of interesting soundscapes and creative musical ideas provided by the ensemble and organized by the soundpainter. In this broad sense, a limited Soundpainting vocabulary and an understanding of the syntax can be a productive constraint, in that it outlines the possibilities for meta-agentic communication.

Indicating Openness

How is openness to contributions from ensemble members achieved in Soundpainting? The answer lies, in part, in the many what-signs that require ensemble members to improvise. When using these particular signs, the soundpainter is requesting immediate action while simultaneously refraining from specifying what addressees should actually do.

In other words, these signs intentionally leave the final selection of what to do and how to do it open for the addressee to decide. Three examples of such signs will be discussed here: [Point To Point], [Scanning], and [Improvise], which all grant the ensemble member a completely free choice of action, but they constrain and condition other aspects of the ensemble's improvisation in different ways, which are discussed below.

Brainstorming and Immediacy with [Scanning] and [Point to Point]

[Scanning] and [Point to Point] are both used as combined what- and when-signs, occupying both the second and fourth slots in the who-what-how-when syntax. In [Point to Point], for instance, the what-gesture is signed first, outside the imaginary box, which prepares the ensemble for the next step. The when-part of the sign is then performed as the soundpainter steps into the box and begins pointing to individual ensemble members: "When pointed to, the performer immediately begins performing, slowly developing her/his choice of a single idea. The type of improvisation is an open choice of the performer. The performer immediately stops performing when the Point is removed" (Thompson, 2006, p. 25).

Similarly, when performing the what-sign in [Scanning], the soundpainter raises either or both arms straight out to their side(s), about a foot above shoulder height. Then, after stepping into the box and beginning to indicate the when-gesture, the soundpainter moves their arm(s) left or right, passing over the heads of the ensemble members. "Performers respond with open improvisation as the Scanning arm passes over them in either direction. Performers stop immediately after the Scanning arm has passed by" (Thompson, 2006, p. 23). If the soundpainter lets their arm(s) rest at one position, as in [Point To Point], ensemble members who are "being scanned" must continue to improvise for as long as the arm remains there.

For the soundpainter, [Point To Point] and [Scanning] are often used to search for content and generate fresh, musical ideas very quickly. In this sense, the signs may constitute a brainstorm from which certain ideas may be selected for further development (by means of the [Continue] sign, the significance of which is discussed further in Chap. 5), and other ideas may be discarded.

How do ensemble members come up with musical ideas when instructed to improvise with signs like [Scanning] and [Point to Point]? There is no single answer to this question. But worth noting is the fact that all responses necessarily are situated; ensemble embers come from many different backgrounds, and they may be inspired or affected by the social and material setting in which the Soundpainting session occurs. Bruno Faria, for instance, has discussed at length how his own background constituted a "horizon of understanding" (2016, p. 139) for his practical and theoretical engagement with Soundpainting; not only were the musical sounds and gestures he could imagine as a performer and ensemble member tied to his personal history of embodied practice as a classically trained flutist, but his conceptualization of improvisation was also shaped by this identity (ibid.).

While ensemble members are free to choose exactly what to do in the context of [Scanning] and [Point to Point], they are also instructed to start and stop at very specific points in time. The implicit fixity from which the openness of [Point to Point] and [Scanning] is distinguished lies in the temporal domain; by starting and stopping ensemble members dynamically, the signs provide a time window that constrains the beginning and the ending of the addressee's actions. In other words, the main constraint for agency in the case of these signs is a temporal one.

For the individual ensemble member, the initiation and termination of actions happen very quickly in [Scanning] and [Point to Point]; they may be pointed to and must begin improvising with only a fraction of a second's notice, and they must be prepared to stop again with similarly short notice. This requires constant attention and commitment, and [Point to Point] and [Scanning] thus epitomize how Soundpainting generates improvisational immediacy. The performative immediacy produced by these signs is key to understanding their generative power. Due to the unpredictability of the soundpainter's movements, ensemble members can never be entirely certain of the timing of their actions. But why is the timing so significant?

In order to answer this question, we need to consider a central mechanism in the psychology of everyday life. The vast majority of human beings internalize social norms and cultural sensibilities throughout their upbringing and life. These internalized structures then, in turn, facilitate and regulate cognition and behavior. According to symbolic interactionism (an influential strand of micro sociology), this process can be understood in the form of an ever-present "generalized other," whom individuals—consciously or unconsciously—imagine responding to their actions (Blumer, 1969). This mental simulation of how others might respond to what we do acts as both an affective compass and a logical guide for action in the social world. The generalized other helps us navigate toward actions that are likely to be understood as relevant and valuable by significant others. The sociologist Howard Becker famously argued that creative acts are composed of two "moments"—the creative moment, in which actions are generated, and the editorial moment, which acts as a filter, where internalized social and artistic conventions modify the creative impulses (Becker, 1982).

For artists or other people doing creative work, a generalized other that becomes an ever-present inner critic can also be dangerous, in the sense that it may weaken or entirely arrest the improvised impulse at the heart of creative action. This is where the immediacy generated by having to respond quickly to signs such as [Scanning] and [Point to Point] becomes relevant; the editorial moment is pushed to the background for a while, and the generalized other is replaced by a specific other (mainly the soundpainter).

The self-critical and normative thought processes may thus be deemphasized, and ideas that, to a lesser extent, are shaped by critical reflection may then emerge. Such immediacy is, however, a double-edged sword; it can lead to a greater number of what we might call musical clichés than would otherwise occur, but it also opens up to qualitatively different and original musical expressions. The use of precomposed material such as an existing piece of music is generally discouraged in the context of Soundpainting signs like [Scanning] and [Point to Point] (Duckert & Rasmussen, 2013, p. 54), and directly copying preexisting music goes against the creative purpose of composition and improvisation. Due to diminished reflexivity, ideas produced in immediate response to the soundpainter's instructions can be closer to the habitual, bodily automations that we have built up through previous experiences.

In my view, however, the danger that musician Derek Bailey (1992, p. 88) associates with the use of clichés in improvisation and art does not apply here; the advantages of the openness that Soundpainting enables more than outweigh the risk of repeating simple musical ideas. Besides, combining otherwise unrelated clichés can become an important source of creative material; imagine a 12-bar blues chord progression played on an electric guitar, combined with dramatic, repeated motifs played on a cello in a parallel key. Add an improvised rap performed in a different meter, and we have a complex, unusual musical assemblage that could become an interesting piece of music.

While this imagined scenario is but one among many possibilities, it shows that remixing clichés and stylistic idioms in the course of performance can be a constructive route to new musical expressions. This is not to say that Soundpainting favors a postmodern ideal of remix and recombination of existing materials as the creative modus operandi. If somewhat recognizable musical styles emerge due to the immediacy of [Scanning] and [Point to Point], these are not something to be feared—they are merely resources that can be refined, dissected, amplified, etc. And Soundpainting provides the tools for this further processing in the form of specific signs, to which I return in Chap. 5. It should suffice for now to say that the improvisational immediacy produced by signs like [Scanning] and [Point to Point] is not something to be feared but should be understood as a potential resource in the creative process.

The Special Case of [Improvise]

Of the signs in Soundpainting that emphasize openness to performer choice, [Improvise], which grants the addressee "the freedom to fully go in any direction they chooses" (Thompson, 2006, p. 33), is an important example. According to Thompson, [Improvise] holds a special position in Soundpainting vocabulary since "it is the only gesture in Soundpainting that indicates the performer has the liberty to do what they desire. Certain other gestures incorporate varying degrees of choice regarding their material though nowhere near the same level as the [Improvise] gesture" (Thompson, quoted by Minors, 2012, p. 146).

All decisions about what to do are left open to the addressee, except only for the fact that something must be done; the ensemble member who was given the [Improvise] sign must perform an action or a series of actions. What makes [Improvise] possible, then, is that addressees commit to doing something. To do nothing (i.e., to continue performing in the exact same way as before) when given the [Improvise] sign would likely be considered counterproductive by experienced soundpainters since it violates the division of labor between ensemble (which provides the ideas and "raw materials") and soundpainter (whose responsibilities are similar to those of the news editor or the record producer). The division of labor will be discussed further in Chap. 4. The freedom bestowed upon an ensemble member by means of the [Improvise] sign is thus predicated on the ensemble member's commitment to take action.

The special status of the [Improvise] sign pertains in particular to the question of when the addressee should stop improvising. Terminations of performer activity are usually indicated implicitly by the soundpainter when they instruct addressees to perform some kind of content, which replaces what they were doing previously. When [Whole Group][Long Tone][Play] is signed, for instance, the ensemble is instructed to play sustained notes. This sustained activity may at a later point in time be replaced by another form of content, as in [Whole Group][Minimalism][Play] ([Minimalism] will be discussed below), or it may be terminated with the [Whole Group][Off] phrase.

While it would likewise be syntactically correct to sign [Brass 1] [Improvise][Slowly Enter] followed 10 seconds later by [Whole group] [Off], that would be considered an immature use of the Soundpainting language since this would effectively cut off the soloist (who is included in the [Whole Group]) just as they are beginning the improvised solo. If an ensemble member has been given the phrase [You][Improvise][Enter Slowly], Soundpainting etiquette, as described by Thompson, prescribes two possibilities for determining when the improvisation should stop: The improviser can end the improvisation on their own, or the soundpainter may use the [Finish Your Idea] sign to indicate to the improvising ensemble member that they should begin to wrap up their solo (Thompson, 2006, p. 45).

During a break at a Soundpainting workshop I attended with Thompson and other soundpainters in Paris in 2016, Thompson recalled a discussion around the [Improvise] sign that had taken place in one of his early Soundpainting ensembles: A musician was displeased with the amount of time that had been allotted for the conclusion of an improvised solo, and [Finish Your Idea] was invented out of respect for "the improviser." As Thompson explains in an instruction video, [Finish Your Idea] is a means of finishing a solo that was initiated with [Improvise] with only a minimal intrusion on the improviser's freedom to conclude their improvised solo on their own terms:

> When you ask someone to [Improvise], that is a full-blown improvisation. That person is probably going to give blood to the composition […]. In Soundpainting, for the respect of the improviser, we do not cut them off or say [Slowly Exit]. There is only one gesture we use, and […] this gesture is [Finish Your Idea]. It is reserved for and only given to the soloist, the improviser. And it gives them as much as a minute and a half to finish what

they are doing, to bring it to a natural conclusion. An improviser can also stop by themselves without a gesture from the soundpainter; it is one of the exceptions of Soundpainting where the improviser, if they feel like their improvisation is over after just one minute, can stop, of course, and wait for the next gesture. (Thompson, 2017, 37:20, my transcription)

This description almost evokes romanticist imagery of an organism that must live, evolve, and come to a "natural conclusion." [Improvise] creates a marked section within the performance, carves out time and space for addressees to pour themselves into the heart of the performance and "give blood," i.e., make significant, "full-blown" contributions. The understanding of improvisation that is embodied in the meaning of the [Improvise] sign thus emphasizes soloing and individual expression, similarly to many forms of jazz music; a section of a composition is reserved for an improvised solo, and the personal style of the soloist may shine through, which establishes a certain figure–ground relationship between the soloist and the rest of the ensemble.

While [Improvise] thus occupies a special status in the Soundpainting language, improvisation is embodied in many other content signs in more or less subtle ways. In the following section, we move on from our discussion of signs that indicate openness and are designed to leave many aspects of agency open to performer choice to signs that indicate certain kinds of musical content. These signs, however, also invite improvisation and interpretation on the part of the ensemble, but in subtler ways.

Indicating Specific Musical Content

Distinct from signs that leave decisions about what and how to play to ensemble members, Soundpainting also contains signs that specify certain kinds of content to be performed, as in the familiar example [Long Tone]. The similar what-sign known as [Hits] also works as a when-sign, being initiated one at a time and instructing addressees to play singular, staccato notes reminiscent of a wind section "hit" in big band jazz. Signs such as [Long Tone] or [Hits] may at first seem to be very simple and specific instructions: Play a sustained note or, conversely, play a very short note. [Long Tone] and [Hits], however, only indicate different sides of a distinction between punctuality and continuity in the temporal dimension, which leaves parameters such as pitch, volume, and timbre open to a performer's choice, as discussed above. Many what-signs share this feature, indicating some type of content while leaving some parameters open as the unmarked side of the distinction about the action to be taken. Such signs include:

- [Pointilism], "arrhythmic, staccato notes and bits of longer notes performed rapidly" (Thompson, 2006, p. 24), which generates a texture of quickly shifting sounds, leaving open decisions about pitch, sound, timbre, volume, etc.;
- [Drone], "a slow undulation, within a small range, between several [Long Tones]" (Thompson, 2010, p. 32), which leaves parameters such as pitch and volume unspecified;
- [Speak], which instructs participants to use their voices for speaking but leaves lyrics, mood, tone, topics, pitch, etc., open to a performer's choice;
- [Melody], which is somewhat self-explanatory but leaves open questions of style, phrasing, tonality, and key; and
- [Extended Techniques], which instructs the addressee to do "something uncharacteristic with your instrument" (Thompson, 2006, p. 31).

Signs like [Long Tone] and [Melody] highlight the primacy of music in the design of the Soundpainting language. Thompson's background, as discussed in Chap. 1, is mainly in music. However, the sign language also has an interdisciplinary scope, as exemplified by signs like [Pointilism], which (although a familiar descriptor of mid-twentieth-century experimental music) is clearly inspired by abstract, visual art. Soundpainting may, however, also be used in other (combinations of) artistic disciplines, including theater and dance, as well as visual art. In these disciplines, the signs that specify content have translated meanings; in dance, for instance, [Long Tone] corresponds to continuous, smooth motion. These interdisciplinary aspects and specifically multidisciplinary content signs such as [Movement] will not be discussed further here but can be studied in *Workbooks 3* and *4* (Thompson, 2014, 2022).

A unique way of specifying content, the [Shapeline] sign does not initiate a sustained action or repeating series of actions but rather requires ensemble members to musically interpret the soundpainter's movements. When the soundpainter steps into the box after having signed [Shapeline], their movements should be interpreted not as symbols with conventional meanings that are detached from the form of the gesture but as visual shapes to be translated into musical sound: "Performers musically perform the physical shape the Soundpainter creates with her/his body – physical graphic notation" (Thompson, 2006, p. 34). While the soundpainter's movements constitute an abstract guide for the musical actions of the ensemble members, responding with musical sound that somehow relates to this "shape" requires some interpretive creativity from ensemble members and thus also involves openness to performer choice.

Some what-signs instruct ensemble members to play repeating patterns, of which [Minimalism] and [Vamp] are perhaps the most obvious examples. [Minimalism] instructs addressees to perform a simple, "continuous, rhythmic cycling of the same several pitches without change" (Thompson, 2006, p. 27), letting addressees choose the specific rhythmic structure (and pitches, if applicable to the performer's instrument) that make up the phrase, but demanding that said content be organized in musical time in a repeating and rhythmically discernible pattern. [Minimalism] does not specify musical meter, and ensemble members may decide to play patterns that follow other meters, such as 4/4, 3/8, 7/4, or do not have a strong sense of musical meter. [Vamp], a "one or two measure (or more) repetitive phrase created as a rhythmic foundation to be built upon" (Thompson, 2010, p. 43), is similar to [Minimalism] but requires the repeating pattern to be defined within a particular musical meter and function, like a rhythmical vamp.

Delving deeper into the degrees of specificity with which the soundpainter may indicate content to be performed by the ensemble, we find signs for rhythm, pitch, key, chord, style, etc. [Rhythm Tap] allows the soundpainter to tap a short rhythmic sequence as a piece of content, specifying rhythm but leaving the open pitch, feeling, etc. Similarly, there is a set of signs known as the [Note] family, which allows for detailed specification of notes as understood in musical notation, i.e., specific durations ranging from whole notes through 32nd notes and higher, tuplets, etc. Pitches C, D, E, F, G, A, and B may be specified with the [Note Mode] sign, which, combined with the [Flat] and [Sharp] signs, supports the specification of all notes in the Western, chromatic 12-note scale. Specific keys or scales can be specified with the [Keys] signs; chords can be specified with the [Chord] sign, which has further options for specifications such as [Major], [Minor], [Diminished], and [Augmented]. As with most what-signs, these can be combined into very long phrases, composing very specific musical content almost exactly as one would do when using conventional musical notation: [Rhythm Tap][With][Note Mode (C, E, G)] will yield a C major triad arpeggiated using the specified rhythm (the important [With] sign is discussed below). Further details for musical articulation may be specified with such how-signs as [Volume Fader], [Legato], and [Staccato], allowing for fine-grained control of how instructed content is to be performed. Composing highly specific musical content is thus entirely possible in Soundpainting. These signs all indicate fixity as opposed to improvisation in their specifications of the action to be carried out by addressees.

However, even with the broad range of what- and how-signs available for instruction, the efficiency of Soundpainting as a medium for conveying highly specific information about conventional aspects of musical content (pitches, duration, articulation, key, modulation, etc.) could arguably be considered inferior to that of standard musical notation, due to the complexity of the gesture combinations one would need to perform to sign the equivalent of a written phrase. Indeed, as Duckert and Rasmussen pointed out to me during my early forays into Soundpainting, the communication of highly detailed instruction using the signs described above is not always the most interesting aspect of Soundpainting. Thompson similarly emphasizes the understanding of live composition as a collaborative process between soundpainter and ensemble, construing Soundpainting as a tool mainly for composing with ideas provided by the ensemble in the course of the performance:

> Of course, I could say 'please give me an f sharp in octave 4', I can sign that if I want to. [...] There's all of that available in the language, but that's not the point of the language. The point of the language is to give a kind of empty box, and then the performer fills it with the content the soundpainter is asking for. (Sabbe & Thompson, 2024, 6:46, my transcription)

The emphasis on real-time production of musical content, which characterizes improvised music, is an important aspect of Soundpainting not only in the discourse of its practitioners but also in the design of the sign language. However, it is also clear that Soundpainting does not deny the value of using precomposed elements altogether. The [Palette] sign specifically refers to precomposed blocks of musical content and is defined in the following way: "Any section of composed and/or rehearsed music. Palettes may range from a few seconds in length to more than 15 minutes and are performed on cue" (Thompson, 2010). The related [Palette Punch] sign is defined along similar lines and is mainly used for short one-time events. [Palette] is usually enumerated, which allows for the use and coexistence of multiple distinct pieces of precomposed/rehearsed content and can be used to initiate performance of predefined musical content at any point during an otherwise largely improvised performance. For instance, a predefined groove can be used as a point of departure, a precomposed section of music can be used as an interlude or a recurring theme throughout a performance, or precomposed strings of words can be used as lyrics for singers, etc. In this way, the [Palette] sign indicates fixity as opposed to improvisation, in whatever form it is precomposed/ rehearsed, yet its timing and even its use obviously relies upon the soundpainter's decisions throughout the performance; the rehearsal of content for a [Palette] does not require the soundpainter to actually ever use the specific [Palette], and furthermore (as we shall discuss further below), the content of a [Palette] may be used in various ways that leave many parameters open to performer choice.

Combining Openness and Constraint

While the [Improvise] sign grants a great degree of freedom to addressees, as discussed earlier, it arguably also entails the largest degree of contingency in Soundpainting; no decisions have been made for the ensemble member who is given the instruction to [Improvise]—except that a significant effort should be made to contribute an improvised solo. The ensemble member can do anything, but since it is impossible to do everything at the same time, they are forced to do something particular and, in so doing, to draw a distinction within the enormous space of possible actions, fully aware that the soundpainter and other ensemble members will be listening and adapting to their improvisation. In this very open situation, Soundpainting provides a tool for mediation of improvisation and constraint: The [With] sign.

Nuanced Constraint Using [With]

[With] is an exception to the syntax in that it cannot be used as a standalone what-sign but is used instead as a "conjunction—a link between gestures" (Thompson, 2006, p. 39). Using open signs like [Improvise] or [Scanning] in conjunction with the [With] sign and one further what-sign allows the soundpainter to specify content to be used in the addressee's improvisation. For instance, the phrase outline [Woodwind 1][Improvise]

[With][Long Tone][Slowly Enter] instructs the first woodwind player to play an improvised solo mainly using sustained notes. [With] is mainly used in this way as a means to constrain entirely open what-signs by linking them to more specific what-signs.

There are several motivations for constraining the improvised agency of addressees using the [With] sign in this way. The soundpainter may seek homogeneity in the sonic result when using open signs addressed to the whole ensemble, as in [Whole Group][Scanning][With][Pointilism] or [Whole Group][Scanning][With][Long Tone], which yield cascades of staccato sounds or sustained notes, respectively. Another reason might be for [With] to be used in cases where the ensemble member is finding the task of improvising difficult, not knowing what to do when faced with the idea that one can do anything. It may, in this latter case, be desirable to reduce the space of possible actions for the ensemble member by introducing some kind of constraint. Phrases like [String 2][Improvise][With] [2 Notes][Slowly Enter], where [Note] is used to specify a limited number of notes with all other parameters (pitches, timbre, rhythm, articulation, etc.) left open to performer choice, effectively constrain the improvisation so that the string player is only allowed to use two out of many possible notes. While this may be a very tight constraint, the instruction to improvise with some limitations in the content may, in fact, enable agency rather than hinder it, even if the instruction appears to involve less freedom for the ensemble member. Similarly, [Without] means the opposite of [With], but can still act as a creative constraint; using [Improvise][Without][Long Tone] as a compound what-sign instructs the addressee to improvise using anything but sustained notes.

A related use of the [With] sign occurs in the context of [Vamp] and [Minimalism], which normally leave decisions about style to addressees. Style can be specified in greater detail when [Vamp] or [Minimalism] are conjoined with the [Feel] sign, as in [You (Bass player)][Vamp][With][Swing][Feel], which instructs the bass player to begin playing a vamp in a swing style. Other musical styles may be specified using the style family of [Classical], [Funk], [Machine/Techno], [March], [Rock], or [Swing] signs, which are all used with the [With] and [Feel] sign, as in [Whole Group][Vamp][With][Rock][Feel], which specifies that the [Vamp] should be a vamp in the style of "rock" music. Terms such as "rock," "classical," or "swing" obviously refer to very broad categories and thus still leave some space for interpretation to the ensemble member—unless a more specific definition of, for instance, "classical" has been defined in rehearsal.

Using [With], an entirely open sign like [Improvise], can be conjoined with the [Palette] sign, essentially giving addressees a precomposed point of departure for their improvised solo. For instance, if [Palette 1] has been defined as a short motif based on ascending thirds and [Palette 2] is another motif based on descending thirds, interesting results could be obtained by signing [String 1][Improvise][With][Palette 1], [String 2] [Improvise][With][Palette 2], [Enter Slowly]. Or by defining other palettes, singers could be given lyrics or words to use as points of departure for their improvisation, percussionists could be given specific rhythms, etc.

All the examples of [With] discussed here may be understood as reentries of the improvisation/fixity distinction into very open instructions, where the open space of possibilities marked by, for instance, [Improvise], [Scanning], or [Point To Point] is once more divided into parameters that are fixed and parameters that are left open. The compound expression [Improvise][With][Long Tone] essentially divides the open space of possible actions assigned with the [Improvise] sign into a set of likely actions (i.e., musical content which, at least as a point of departure, is based on sustained notes) and unlikely actions (e.g., staccato sounds and extended techniques).

The examples of this figure of reentry mentioned thus far all indicate the reentry of fixity into improvisation, i.e., using a constraint that reduces the space of possible actions from the addressee to configure the category of content with which addressees should begin to build their improvisation. However, the other side of the distinction can also be indicated by using the [Change] sign (which will be discussed further below) to widen the field of possibilities, insisting that new content should be performed every time a new iteration occurs. An example would be the use of the compound what-sign [Point To Point][With][Change] which instructs ensemble members to perform something different every time they are pointed to.

What motivates the use of this particular strategy? Other than the aesthetic desire for a performance with ever-changing musical expressions, one particular motivation may be pedagogical. In several interviews, Thompson has mentioned encountering "a little resistance" to Soundpainting from musicians who are very familiar with markedly improvised music (such as professional jazz musicians): "Jazz is rich in improvisation and jazz musicians spend a great deal of time perfecting their ability to perform a solo improvisation as well as collective improvisation. When I teach Soundpainting to a Jazz group, sometimes I meet a little resistance from a few players who do not like being signed" (Minors, 2012). When asked about his strategies for Soundpainting workshops for participants with varying degrees of experience with improvisation, Thompson specifically referred to his use of the compound what-sign [Point To Point][With][Change]:

> [When teaching] people who are skeptical because they know everything about improvisation and think "what in the world could I teach them," one of the things that tears down those walls is when I say [Point To Point][With][Change]. So everytime I point to you, you give me something different, everytime it is a different choice. And I will go after a few people over and over to see how much they can vary and change their ideas. It does not take too long before they repeat themselves. (Thompson, personal communication, 25 May 2016)

The content offered has to differentiate itself from what was played only moments ago, and this operation repeats on each iteration, yielding perhaps the clearest example of how Soundpainting can enforce the reentry of improvisation into an already improvised process, achieving a continually changing series of musical expressions. Ultimately, this point leads to the topic of recursion in Soundpainting, something that will be discussed further in Chap. 5.

In summary, what-signs are generally designed to be open to performer choice or to specify certain kinds of preexisting sonic content, usually by reference to stylistic idioms or formal concepts of music theory. As one progresses further into Soundpainting and learns how signs can be combined in various ways, it becomes clear that interesting results can be achieved by combining these categories; improvisation can be constrained creatively within a particular, structural element, or interesting outcomes can be achieved by exploring the boundaries of stylistic idioms and preexisting content. Exploring these intricacies through dialogue between soundpainter and ensemble is a recipe for rich and creative interactions. The next chapter takes a closer look at the social and interactive aspect of such dialogues.

REFERENCES

Bailey, D. (1992). *Improvisation: Its Nature and Practice in Music*. The British Library National Sound Archive.
Becker, H. S. (1982). *Art Worlds*. University of California Press.
Biskjaer, M. M., & Halskov, K. (2014). Decisive Constraints as a Creative Resource in Interaction Design. *Digital Creativity, 25*(1), 27–61. https://doi.org/10.1080/14626268.2013.855239
Blumer, H. (1969). *Symbolic Interactionism: Perspective and Method*. University of California Press.
Christoffersen, E. E. (2011). Spilleregler og benspænd. *Peripeti, 8*(16) Article 16. https://doi.org/10.7146/peri.v8i16.8259
Duckert, K., & Rasmussen, G. (2013). *Sammenspil og improvisation med Soundpainting*. Edition Wilhelm Hansen.
Elster, J. (2000). *Ulysses Unbound: Studies in Rationality, Precommitment, and Constraints*. Cambridge University Press.
Faria, B. (2016). *Exercising Musicianship Anew Through Soundpainting: Speaking Music Through Sound Gestures*. Lund University.
Kieserling, A. (1999). *Kommunikation unter Anwesenden: Studien über Interaktionssysteme*. Suhrkamp Verlag.
Minors, H. J. (2012). Reassessing the Thinking Body in Soundpainting. *How Performance Thinks*, 142–148.
Sabbe, J., & Thompson, W. (Directors). (2024, July 17). *Walter Thompson Interview* [Video recording]. YouTube. https://www.youtube.com/watch?v=Bbuq936ZVrQ
Thompson, W. (2006). *Soundpainting: The Art of Live Composition, Workbook 1*. Self-Published.
Thompson, W. (2010). *Soundpainting: The Art of Live Composition, Workbook 2*. Self-Published.
Thompson, W. (2014). *Soundpainting: The Art of Live Composition, Workbook 3*.
Thompson, W. (Director). (2017). *Soundpainting—Lesson 1—Walter Thompson* [Video recording]. YouTube. https://www.youtube.com/watch?v=YJQf0MDsNaA
Thompson, W. (2022). *Soundpainting: The Art of Live Composition, Workbook 4*.
Vidal Belda, O. (2021). *Componiendo con soundpainting en el aula de música. Un estudio de casos colectivo sobre creación sonora colaborativa* (p. 1) [http://purl.org/dc/dcmitype/Text, Universitat de València]. https://dialnet.unirioja.es/servlet/tesis?codigo=301655

CHAPTER 4

Cocreation: Distributing Agency in Interaction

The first time one attends a Soundpainting performance, one of the first impressions will likely be the way in which the ensemble is organized physically: Members of the ensemble are distributed in physical space around the soundpainter, usually in a semicircle pattern, each ensemble member facing the soundpainter. Similar to choir or orchestra settings, ensemble members are expected to pay close attention to the soundpainter's gestural instructions and be able to maintain eye contact with the soundpainter. Maintaining this line of communication produces a sense of liveness and excitement for the participants, which is part of Soundpainting's appeal.

The Social Nature of Authorship in Soundpainting

At first glance, the performance might also suggest a hierarchical division of labor—a group of workers following orders from a leader—which tends to run counter to the notions of democracy and equality often associated with improvised music. As a scholar and practitioner of Soundpainting, I have often been confronted with the misconception that only the soundpainter is really improvising, since they instruct the ensemble on what to do. While the soundpainter does have different responsibilities from those of ensemble members—especially when compared to more explicitly egalitarian forms of improvised music—such criticism often fails to realize that,

© The Author(s), under exclusive license to Springer Nature
Singapore Pte Ltd. 2024
A. Eskildsen, *Soundpainting*, Palgrave Studies in Sound,
https://doi.org/10.1007/978-981-96-1690-9_4

due to the inherent semantic openness of many Soundpainting signs (as discussed in Chap. 3), ensemble members are required to come up with their own ideas and contribute to the co-creative endeavor of the performance. Emphasizing this collaborative nature in her discussion of authorship in Soundpainting, Helen Julia Minors has thus proposed "that each participant in a Soundpainting work be accredited equally in credits" (Minors, 2020, p. 131). This seems to contrast with Thompson's written statement about ownership:

> Many people ask: "When you compose a Soundpainting, who does it belong to - whose composition is it?" The answer is simple: It's yours! You are the one composing - creating the piece in the moment utilizing Soundpainting gestures to indicate very specific and detailed instructions to be performed. You make the choices of what material to compose with and how to develop it. You are the one creating the architecture and momentum of the piece. If you have Soundpainted a concert, a CD, a radio show, a film, etc. all of these Soundpaintings are your compositions and the title of composer belongs to you. (Thompson, 2010, p. 15)

When it comes to recognizing the creative contributions of participants, Minors's point is an important one: Ensemble members in Soundpainting are often required to improvise and develop musical materials and ideas on a level beyond that of a traditional performer of a work of music. To some extent, this reflects twentieth-century developments in experimental music vis-à-vis Cage, Brown, Cardew, and similar composers, where the distinction between composer and performer is maintained, but with new expectations for both categories of participants qua the notion of the open work. Rather than "prescribing a defined *time-object* whose materials, structuring and relationships are calculated and arranged in advance" (Nyman, 1974, p. 3), experimental music's early composers were interested in "outlining a *situation* in which sounds may occur, a *process* of generating action (sounding or otherwise), a *field* delineated by certain compositional 'rules'" (ibid.). Performers, in this tradition, are relied upon to interpret, make decisions, come up with musical materials, and, in some cases, even to "invent [...] particular instruments or electronic systems" (ibid.). These expectations grant performers a level of freedom and co-responsibility like that of improvised musical practices in and beyond advanced mid-century jazz. For further discussion of the intertwined histories of jazz, improvised music, and experimentalism, see Lewis (1996, 2008), Feisst (2016), Kim (2012), and Piekut (2011, 2014).

Among improvisers who emphasize freely improvised group interaction, egalitarian ideals in which "creative authority [...] is decentralized" (Belgrad, 2016, p. 290) continue to thrive, resonating with Minors's argument concerning the equal attribution of credit across participants in Soundpainting. But Soundpainting is not free improvisation in the sense that hierarchical modes of an interactional organization or predistributed roles are entirely abandoned; one of the defining features of Soundpainting is the distinction between the soundpainter and the ensemble. These roles, however, transcend traditional notions of the composer as the sole author and the performer as detached from the creative effort. If the soundpainter's role is to be understood as an authorial one, as per Thompson's statements, the notion of authorship should be clarified, in my view, to reflect the inherently social and interactive nature of creative labor in Soundpainting.

It is instructive here to turn to Jason Toynbee's notion of "social authorship" in music (Toynbee, 2000). Toynbee has synthesized an interesting reconceptualization of musical creativity, combining Mikhail Bakhtin's notion of dialogism in literary works and Umberto Eco's idea of semiotic codes. In Toynbee's view, "music needs to be understood as an ensemble of coded voices" (Toynbee, 2012, p. 164). "Coded voices" is an abstract, theoretical category that encompasses a wide range of musical materials. Examples include culturally recognizable sounds such as "the sliding tones of the early Billie Holiday, say, or a baroque harpsichord in busy chime" (ibid.) as well as formal rules qua music theory, such as "the movement structure of the concerto or the metrical organization of the British electronic dance genre called grime" (ibid.). Even though Toynbee did not have Soundpainting in mind but sought to conceptualize musical creativity in a broad sense, his notion of the social author corresponds quite beautifully with the soundpainter; "the author's work can be understood as the identification of coded voices and their arrangement in meaningful dialogue" (Toynbee, 2012, p. 165). The soundpainter identifies useful or interesting contributions from the ensemble and (re)arranges the musical materials to create a cohesive arrangement of sounds.

As Toynbee points out, in contexts such as classical or popular music, "the collocation of coded voices is highly conventional" (ibid.); many ways of arranging coded voices will already be given as stylistic conventions before the creative process begins. But in Soundpainting, the soundpainter often does not know which coded voices they will be able to work with, and the arrangement of coded voices will often be experimental, an emergent property rather than a predefined form or distribution. This is achievable, in part, due to Soundpainting's conventions and design. This chapter focuses on the responsibilities and possibilities of the soundpainter and the ensemble in Soundpainting-based interactions. Whereas Toynbee's theoretical contentions concern rethinking the sociality of an individual, musical creator, Soundpainting is impossible without participants listening, observing, and reacting to one another responsibly. In this sense, Soundpainting embodies an "ethics of cocreation" (Fischlin et al., 2013).

From a practical, microsociological point of view, being a soundpainter constitutes a distinct category that incorporates composing, conducting, improvising, editing, teaching, supporting, etc. Similarly, being a member of a Soundpainting ensemble involves unique expectations that differ from those placed upon artists in most other settings. With no creative contributions and commitment from the ensemble, the soundpainter's task becomes meaningless, and they can wave their arms all day long with no satisfactory result. Conversely, if the soundpainter fails to display musical sensibility toward the contributions of ensemble members, fails to conduct the ensemble with an editorial outlook to the performance as a whole, or simply does not communicate well by performing the gestures clearly, the ensemble will find it difficult to perform in a creative and meaningful way.

This chapter explores how Soundpainting establishes and builds upon this fundamental interdependency between participants. First, the static distribution of agency between soundpainter and ensemble is discussed in terms of the possibilities for emergent interplay between the two that Soundpainting engenders. Second, the ways in which Soundpainting allows for dynamic distributions of agency in the course of performance are discussed, highlighting how subgroups within the ensemble may be created on the fly and musical dialogues and interactions between ensemble members may be facilitated.

Static Distributions of Agency

The distinction between soundpainter and ensemble is one of the most fundamental principles of Soundpainting; one participates in Soundpainting as either the soundpainter or as a member of the ensemble. This setup characterizes conducted improvisation in general.

Beyond their different placements in the physical performance space, the distinction between these two roles entails that soundpainter and ensemble have distinct sets of fundamental responsibilities, which remain in place throughout the performance. In other words, Soundpainting employs a static distribution of potentials for agency between soundpainter and ensemble.

The staticity is functional and not tied to individual persons, in the sense that while the soundpainter can sign one of the ensemble members to take over as soundpainter and switch places with them, the form and function of the soundpainter/ensemble distinction remains in place, demarcated by the physical distribution of participants and embodied in the ensemble's sustained orientation toward the new soundpainter.

This staticity of the distinction between ensemble and soundpainter is important, since it means that participants can rely upon it when other social aspects of the performance are fluid or dynamic; ensemble members can rely upon the soundpainter to provide organizational scaffolding and make editorial decisions when things get chaotic, and the soundpainter can rely upon ensemble members to make intelligent musical decisions and fill out the gaps in the heat of the moment. The differentiation of tasks and expectations for soundpainter and ensemble is thus a crucial feature of Soundpainting.

In my own expierence teaching Soundpainting workshops, participants usually understand how to contribute as an ensemble member much better when they have tried stepping into the soundpainter's shoes and felt how dependent one is on the ensemble's commitment. Conversely, soundpainters who communicate clearly by ensuring that their instructions are understandable and achievable from the ensemble member's point of view are more likely to achieve a meaningful dialogue with the ensemble.

The Soundpainter

In order to participate as a soundpainter, a participant must be able to perform the Soundpainting gestures in a clear and understandable way, since ensemble members must be able to observe and understand the gestural communication. This is not simply a matter of rehearsing the gestures but also of maintaining awareness of the behavior and perceptual orientation of ensemble members. In order to retain the attention of the ensemble members, the soundpainter needs to maintain frequent eye contact across the ensemble and give minor body language cues that affirm the mutual attentiveness. In my own experience teaching Soundpainting workshops for musicians who have little experience in improvisation, an affirmative and supportive attitude is a crucial condition for success, especially in the early stages.

As discussed in Chap. 3, Soundpainting may conceivably be used to compose only with musical materials that are defined by the soundpainter (either in situ, using specific what-signs to specify musical content, or prior to performance, by means of the [Palette] sign). But the practices I have participated in and observed in Soundpainting workshops and the published instruction materials mentioned previously all emphasize a collaborative ethics that emphasizes the soundpainter's reliance upon input from the ensemble:

> Soundpainting is collaborative in the sense that the soundpainter initiates the phrase, listens to the result [...], and then makes a decision about what to do next. The composition progresses in that way, live composing – it is unpredictable. (Thompson, 2017, 25:02, my transcription)

This entails that the soundpainter should dare to provide instructions that are open to performer choice, listen closely to the musical input offered by the ensemble, and build a composition in real time using that input. While the soundpainter appears to be in a more powerful position than the ensemble members, using that position to rule a musical dictatorship where ensemble members are stripped of any freedom, i.e., only using signs with a minimal degree of openness (such as the note family, [Rhythm Tap], and fully precomposed [Palettes]) and describing the desired content and musical parameters with a high degree of specificity, is not, in my view, the most interesting or useful application of the Soundpainting language.

All the teachers with whom I have studied Soundpainting emphasized that the soundpainter should open up, listen to, develop, support, and transform the musical ideas that are provided by ensemble members. According to this logic, if the soundpainter did not work with the material provided by the ensemble but merely stuck to their own ideas, there would be little use for Soundpainting, as one could simply provide written scores and/or instructions during rehearsals.

When thus electing to use signs like [Scanning], [Point To Point], [Minimalism], or [Improvise], which all emphasize ensemble member improvisation, the soundpainter does not know in advance what they are going to get from the ensemble. This indeterminacy is one of the particular joys of Soundpainting; during a break at a Soundpainting session in Paris, Thompson explained to me that he always hopes to be surprised by what ensemble members bring to the table when instructed to improvise. In turn, when ensemble members begin to improvise, the soundpainter is expected to pay close attention to the ensemble's actions, figuring out how the next instruction should connect to what is currently going on. Discussing how to assess the quality of a soundpainter (beyond being able to perform the gestures clearly), Thompson and Minors emphasize active, peripheral listening, combined with the ability to make reasoned, editorial decisions in the moment (2015b, 8:40).

The idea of stepping back and listening is embodied in the Soundpainting syntax; the soundpainter is required to physically step back after having signed a phrase. Stepping out of the imaginary box and letting the ensemble carry out their instructions, the soundpainter is automatically given time to listen, process what is going on, and consider the next step. The ability of a soundpainter to listen to the ensemble and make editorial decisions is crucial for the performance to flow, and the soundpainter is an important nexus that may allow interesting, emergent content to flourish in the interaction between participants. In addition to requiring sensitivity to the ensemble's input on the soundpainter's part, Soundpainting also provides signs with which the soundpainter may sustain, support, sort, transform, and generally use such perturbations as building blocks as the performance progresses. Such transformative operations will be discussed in Chap. 5.

Bruno Faria describes the soundpainter's ability to listen constructively as an "essential quality" and relates it to a particularly improvisational mode of being, illustrated by a depiction of the expertise of his fellow soundpainter and flutist, Sabine Vogel:

> Perhaps due to her professionalism as a flutist–improviser, I understood that her way of soundpainting was pervaded by deep listening, a mode of engagement borne of the intentionality of making something with a sound. The

time she took to listen to the expressions I was constructing, sometimes with a lowered gaze, looking at [the] floor, or straight through me instead of at me, without making direct eye contact, before having made a decision concerning the direction she would like our performance to take, I understood as a particular identity trait. To me, it disclosed an aspect of tranquility when dealing with the unforeseen of improvisation, and an openness to what a fellow improviser has to say—both essential qualities for the practice of soundpainting. (Faria, 2016, p. 160)

In insisting on a division of labor between ensemble members who provide content and the soundpainter who has an editorial function, Soundpainting derives its improvisational creativity and inventiveness from the interaction between the two. In the views of leading soundpainters, as we have seen, Soundpainting is not supposed to be one-way communication. On the contrary, when practiced according to the collaborative ethics mentioned above, Soundpainting is an example par excellence of how improvised music stages and draws upon what the sociologist Niklas Luhmann termed double contingency (Luhmann, 2013); the soundpainter depends on the ensemble but does not know how ensemble members will respond to their signs, and ensemble members depend on coordination and instruction from the soundpainter but do not know which signs and phrases they will receive or how their input will fit into the group's collective output. The inherent unpredictability of this doubly contingent situation is productive; it can produce excitement and nerve in the interaction, giving focus to the commitment of participants. In order to harness the creative results of the dialogue, Soundpainting offers methods of capturing and developing the input from the ensemble, which will be discussed further in Chap. 5.

Soundpainting is thus not an example of raw double contingency; with the static distribution of agency between a soundpainter and an ensemble, there are many possible scenarios and contingencies that participants need not consider, compared to more egalitarian approaches to free improvisation. Like other aspects of Soundpainting, this constraint may be construed as both a strength and a weakness. There is no point in arguing that Soundpainting is somehow artistically better than more egalitarian forms of improvised music, but it is clear that the social asymmetry in Soundpainting allows the social interaction to react decisively to itself and thus promote interesting results.

The Ensemble

One of the striking assertions about Soundpainting's scope of application that often gets mentioned is the idea that "anybody can be a part of a Soundpainting group" (Thompson & Minors, 2015c, 5:38). Duckert and Rasmussen argue a similar point in their tutorial for music teachers, in that students of all skill levels should be able to respond to an open-ended instruction, such as [Whole Group][Improvise][With][Long tone(s)] [Play], which challenges the student to improvise at their personal level of skill (Duckert & Rasmussen, 2013, p. 49). Vidal Belda's (2021) research on the application of Soundpainting at different educational levels empirically supports the notion of Soundpainting's broad applicability.

This does not mean, however, that in Soundpainting, ensemble members are entirely free to perform as they see fit. As discussed previously, ensemble members should understand the syntax and the meanings of the signs being used and act according to the soundpainter's instructions. It is also obvious that a group of untrained children will be able to create very different performances from a professional string quartet or an amateur big band. But beyond this, what does it mean to be an ensemble member, what is expected of the ensemble?

During my participation in workshops by Thompson, Duckert, and Rasmussen, I initially participated as an ensemble member and only later progressed to taking on the role of the soundpainter, as is probably the case for most other beginning practitioners of Soundpainting. As an ensemble member, it became clear that one is expected first and foremost to show commitment, i.e., simply to begin acting when instructed to by the soundpainter. If the soundpainter cannot trust ensemble members to fulfill this expectation, "everything falls apart," as Duckert and Rasmussen explained. If ensemble members refuse to respond to the soundpainter's instructions, the authority invested in the role of the soundpainter crumbles, and interactions based on Soundpainting break down.

What also became clear during my early fieldwork was that ensemble members are always expected to continue performing according to their last instruction until they are addressed again. Recall one of the the ground rules mentioned in Chap. 1: "When in doubt, don't lay out! No matter what, don't stop playing unless you are clearly cut off by the Soundpainter" (Thompson, 2006, p. 8). Of course, situations where performers do not understand the meanings of the soundpainter's signs can and do occur. In these cases, Soundpainting actually provides a sign called [Performer

Doesn't Understand], which—as an exception—is signed not by the soundpainter but by an ensemble member in case "the performer didn't see or doesn't understand the gesture(s) signed and is asking the Soundpainter to re-sign the gesture(s)" (Thompson, 2006, p. 8). According to Thompson's instructions, however, this sign may only be used during rehearsal (ibid.); in concert situations, ensemble members are expected to begin performing when instructed to, even if they do not understand all signs in the phrase.

This leads us to a general and important point regarding the responsibility of ensemble members: The commitment of ensemble members to action should generally take priority over self-percieved mistakes or misunderstandings. In situations where an ensemble member comes to believe that they have misunderstood the soundpainter's signs, for instance, performing [Pointilism] as the rest of the ensemble begins to perform [Long Tone], the ensemble member should continue performing rather than change their course of action to fall in line with the rest of the ensemble. The general rule in Soundpainting is that ensemble members should instead commit to their original understanding of the soundpainter's instruction: "If you accidentally come in with [Pointilism] when the Soundpainter signed [Long Tone], stick with [Pointilism] instead of switching to [Long Tone]. It will be stronger musically than sneaking out and sneaking back in with [Long Tone]. Don't purposely try to achieve this, but if it happens, stay with your choice and wait for the next sign to get back on track" (Thompson, 2006, p. 8). In an interview with Helen Julia Minors, Thompson elaborated on the reasoning behind this rule:

> It is much more interesting and challenging to Soundpaint with the so-called mistake than to acknowledge one has been made. My experience has been that composing with the mistake is quite often a more interesting direction to take the composition than any I could think of. Picasso, Miles Davis, Anthony Braxton, among many other composers acknowledge the so-called "mistake" as an opportunity to discover new material and not as a road block. I share this belief and have made it an important part of the basic philosophy of Soundpainting. (Minors, 2012, p. 147)

The idea of embracing the creative potential of "the mistake" is a common trope in the discourse of jazz musicians, and Soundpainting employs a similar idea that "there are no mistakes" (Thompson, 2006, p. 8). Such statements have led some scholars of (jazz) improvisation to contend "that there are no mistakes per se" (Bertinetto, 2016, p. 86) and that "even unintentional 'mistakes' can be artistic resources" (Bertinetto, 2016, p. 91). However, in dissolving the notion of the mistake, such theories fail to acknowledge the observation that in jazz practice, actions that are perceived as mistakes are often simply ignored by other participating performers (Dempsey, 2008). The social interaction in such cases simply does not connect to the action, discarding it as a perturbation that did not affect the cycle of mutual observation and coordination.

In some cases, artistic performances that are perceived as erroneous due to deviation from established artistic conventions may have wider repercussions for a musician's standing in an artistic community (Becker, 1982, p. 33). This is what the often-mentioned notion of "risk" in the field of improvisation studies entails. Peter J. Martin's "art worlds"-inspired discussion of renowned jazz musician Charlie Parker's career showed how Parker experienced "public humiliation" and discontent from fellow musicians in his early career for performances that were judged by established elders in the jazz community as not living up to "accepted technical and aesthetic standards" (Martin, 2002, p. 144). Evidently, it is empirically incorrect to say that "there are no mistakes" in jazz improvisation. Even if the categorization of actions as mistakes is understood to be socially negotiated (as Bertinetto, Dempsey, and Martin would likely all agree), improvised music nonetheless does involve a possibility of social failure that is real for the participants.

Rather than dismissing the idea of mistakes, then, the more interesting question about mistakes concerns how useful/productive/interesting mistakes are distinguished from useless/unproductive/dull ones. For Martin, this distinction would be drawn by elders in an artistic community according to broadly accepted aesthetic conventions (something which is anticipated by participants themselves as they perform). For Bertinetto, there is no such distinction, since the implied ethical imperative requires the group of performers to "creatively shape a different normative order, which works for the new, previously unexpected, situation" (Bertinetto, 2016, p. 91).

This does not accurately describe what happens in Soundpainting, which incorporates a more pragmatic understanding of mistakes where "interesting" mistakes are selected for further development and other mistakes are not pointed out as mistakes but simply discarded. What distinguishes Soundpainting from other forms of improvisation, then, lies in the handling of "mistakes." The rules of Soundpainting explicitly clearly assign the responsibility for drawing this distinction to the soundpainter.

This centralization of editorial responsibility potentially relieves ensemble members of the fear of failure as long as they act when instructed to; for ensemble members, Soundpainting clearly prioritizes commitment to (sustained) action over the risk of making mistakes. This is the case especially when ensemble members are instructed to improvise through open content signs since they are then expected to come up with a creative "offer" (Thompson & Minors, 2015a, 32:07), providing musical content for the soundpainter to work with. This expectation of commitment and being willing to offer creative ideas and materials illustrates how Soundpainting is predicated on the notion that ensemble members provide the actual content of the performance and that they produce the building blocks with which the soundpainter may do their "live composing."

When given [Improvise], [Scanning], or another similarly open whatsign, addressees are thus forced to decide what to do. While allowing ensemble members to take an active part in creating the performance as it unfolds, the contingency of this choice, of the freedom to do anything, can, of course, be difficult to handle. The sometimes paralyzing notion of complete freedom to choose among all possible courses of action is real and of particular concern for those who teach and study improvisation.

In order to render ensemble members more likely to confine to Soundpainting's rules about commitment, then, a mechanism for the reduction of this contingency is needed. Specifically, the ensemble members need to trust the soundpainter to take responsibility for the editorial aspect of the performance. In other words, the ensemble's trust and confidence in the soundpainter is crucial. As we shall see in Chap. 5, the ensemble entrusts the soundpainter to evaluate and deal competently with what the ensemble offers, a task that entails discarding content perceived as uninteresting or destructive and supporting/developing content perceived as interesting or constructive. In this sense, the responsibility for the aesthetic evaluation of one's actions is, at least in part, lifted from the ensemble member and assigned to the soundpainter. This reduces contingency for ensemble members, improving the commitment to agency and the ensuing generation of interesting, precipitate content.

Dynamic Distributions of Agency

While the distribution of agency between soundpainter and ensemble remains static throughout a performance, further distinctions between ensemble members will be drawn in different ways as performances unfold. Not only can the ensemble be divided into subgroups, but the language is also designed to stage different kinds of relations between the musical actions taken by different ensemble members—relations of contrast, synchronicity, support, tension, etc. This is the reason why, as Duckert and Rasmussen have demonstrated (2016), Soundpainting can be an important tool for training and developing skills in ensemble playing.

Two aspects of the way in which Soundpainting distributes agency within the ensemble will be discussed here: First, the drawing of distinctions between ensemble members in each of the soundpainter's phrases qua the mandatory who-signs will be discussed, including an example of how random distinctions and groupings within the ensemble are generated through the [Play Can't Play] sign. Second, signs that imply varying degrees of openness and fixity in the relations between ensemble members are discussed, including [Synchronize], [Match], [Relate To], as well as the aforementioned [Improvise], which entails distinguishing an improvising soloist from the rest of the ensemble.

Intra-ensemble Relations

Beyond the distinction between soundpainter and ensemble, Soundpainting usually draws further distinctions within the ensemble using the mandatory who-signs. The who-signs coordinate the assignment of future agency to specific participants, determining which ensemble members are going to respond to the soundpainter's phrases and which ensemble members are going to continue performing according to earlier instructions. The most common who-signs indicate either the whole ensemble ([Whole Group]), groupings according to musical instrument ([Brass], [Percussion], [Strings], [Vocalists], [Woodwinds], [Electronics], etc.), specific ensemble members within a group ([Brass 1] or [Strings 3], for instance), custom subgroups defined before the beginning of the performance ([Groups]), one or more ensemble members singled out during performance ([You]—simply pointing out one or more ensemble members), or all ensemble members who were not addressed in the preceding phrase ([Rest of Group]). Additionally, in multidisciplinary Soundpainting, there are other who-signs such as [Actors], [Musicians], [Dancers], and so on.

As mentioned in Chap. 2 regarding the Soundpainting syntax, the who-signs are mandatory; when providing instructions for the ensemble, the soundpainter is always forced to draw a distinction between ensemble members, indicating which ensemble members are currently being addressed. In Soundpainting, agency is thus always assigned to certain participants, and it is always clear who will be acting in response to a given Soundpainting phrase.

Some what-signs delay and randomize the drawing of this distinction, however. The [Scanning] and [Point To Point] signs draw dynamic and immediate distinctions between who is and who is not performing after the soundpainter has stepped into the box, as discussed in Chap. 3. [Play Can't Play] further delays the differentiation of the ensemble, randomizing the composition of a number of subgroups within the ensemble:

> [Play Can't Play] is a series of Cells (entrances) where the performer chooses one Cell, and at the initiation of their Cell, performs without relating to the other performers – as if they are the only one in the room. [...] [Play Can't Play] is a chance gesture and a search gesture. It is a very rich gesture yielding many compositional possibilities. You (the Soundpainter) do not know what you will receive from the performers; it's a surprise! (Thompson, 2010, p. 39)

The practical use of [Play Can't Play], i.e., how ensemble members should respond to the sign, is described in detail in Thompson's *Workbook 2* (Thompson, 2010, p. 39) and will not be discussed here. However, the "many compositional possibilities" mentioned above arise from two chance aspects of [Play Can't Play]: First, [Play Can't Play] randomizes the creation of subgroups and thus facilitates the emergence of unconventional groupings that do not adhere to traditional distinctions between instrument groups or performers belonging to different disciplines (such as instrumentalists vs. singers). Second, with the instruction to perform "as if they are the only one in the room," [Play Can't Play] aims to generate contrasting, composite musical expressions where performers have not had the chance to adapt to what others are doing, since performers who chose the same cell begin to play at the exact same time. In practice, members of an ensemble will often adapt to one another consciously or unconsciously as they perform together (in terms of volume, tempo, style, intonation, or other musical parameters). [Play Can't Play] aims to circumvent this tendency, directly staging unpredictable combinations of performers and musical content. These aspects of improvised interaction will be discussed further below, including the implicit and explicit specifications of relations between the agency of different ensemble members.

Content Developed Through Interaction

While enforcing distinctions between those who will be carrying out instructions embedded in specific phrases and those who will not, Soundpainting does not prescribe any general rules for whether or how ensemble members should act in relation to one another. In insisting that ensemble members mainly focus their attention on the soundpainter, the question of whether and how ensemble members should relate to each other is de-emphasized; constant attention to the soundpainter's gestures is required for the distinction between soundpainter and ensemble to achieve the functional significance that distinguishes conducted improvisation from other forms of improvised music. This tends to move questions about the forms of musical relations between the actions of ensemble members to the background.

Some Soundpainting signs, however, are intended to affect the level of conscious attention to the relationship between ensemble members. Soundpainting thus allows for the soundpainter to specify different ways in which ensemble members should attend and relate to one another, mainly with the [Synchronize], [Match], and [Relate To] signs. These signs specify varying degrees of fixity and openness regarding how ensemble members are expected to relate to one another as they perform.

Given a Soundpainting performance where [Brass 1][Minimalism][Play] has been signed, and [Brass 1] is performing, the soundpainter may sign [Brass 2][Synchronize][With][Brass 1][Slowly Enter], which would require [Brass 2] to imitate [Brass 1], performing in a way that is as close as possible to a verbatim copy of what [Brass 1] is doing. [Brass 2] is required to duplicate not only the rhythmic structure of the ostinato but also the specific pitches, dynamics, and so forth—to the extent that duplication is possible in the specific situation. Regarding the use of [Synchronize] in different situations, Thompson notes the creative possibilities arising from the inherent limitations in the ability of performers to duplicate different kinds of musical content:

In some instances, synchronization may easily be replicated, but in others, because of the complexity of the material to be Synchronized, the performer Synchronizing may have to search around [...]. In complex synchronizations there are times when only searching will take place – this is a very effective use of [Synchronize]. (Thompson, 2006, p. 35)

Whereas the above example where the content performed is simple and repetitive (cf. [Minimalism]), it may be relatively easy to imitate, yielding a situation where [Brass 1] and [Brass 2] are performing the same content and now constitute a small unit within the ensemble. On the other hand, if [Brass 1] were performing a more unpredictable kind of content that does not repeat (had they, for example, been instructed to perform [Pointilism] or to [Improvise]), the [Synchronize] sign would still require [Brass 2] to predict and copy [Brass 1]'s actions to the best of their ability, effectively engendering a relation where the addressee follows another ensemble member in a perhaps more complex and chaotic way (what Thompson refers to as "searching" above).

Distinct from the imitative relation implied by [Synchronize], [Match] instructs addressees to perform the same kind of content as other ensemble members but avoid copying exactly what they are playing, i.e., to perform as if they had been given the same what-sign: "If [Brass 1] is playing a high-pitched [Long Tone] and the Soundpainter signs [Rest Of Group] [Match][Play], the rest of the group would perform a [Long Tone] of their choosing—matching content only and not the exact pitch" (Thompson, 2010, p. 36). [Match] thus implies a relation of similarity between the agency of addressees, but only in terms of the kind of content to be performed.

[Relate To] is different from [Synchronize] and [Match], requiring that addressees perform in a way that "relates to" other ensemble members, leaving open exactly what it means to "relate." [Relate To] does not specify content but indicates instead where the addressee should direct their attention and to whom their playing should be related. For instance, if the soundpainter has signed [Strings 1][Improvise][Play], [Strings 2] [Relate To][Strings 1][Slowly Enter] instructs [Strings 2] to somehow perform in relation to how [Strings 1] is performing. Thompson explains how ensemble members can interpret this instruction in different ways:

> [Relate To] is sort of a free gesture, and you can [Relate To] how you want. It is up to you how you make your relationship. [...] You can be supportive

if you [Relate To] somebody […] or you can contrast what they are doing. You could be an anarchist and just bury it. The relationship is wide open, and it does not mean "do an accompaniment". It can be that, but it could also be a contrast. (Thompson, 2017, 9:28, my transcription)

[Relate To] thus frames the implicit improvisation required from the addressee in terms of an open, social relation with another performer. This could be observed as a dialogical relation where both interactants are expected to act in relation to one another; yet in the example above, [Strings 1] is improvising and has not been instructed to relate to [Strings 2], so no relationality is required explicitly in the opposite direction. However, [Strings 1] may decide to adapt or respond to [Strings 2]'s performance qua their freedom as an improviser. Alternatively, the soundpainter may also sign [Strings 1][Strings 2][Relate To][Slowly Enter], which leaves completely open what to play, essentially requiring [Strings 1] and [Strings 2] to improvise while continually relating to one another's actions.

A particularly interesting example of how certain signs imply a specific relation between ensemble members pertains to the [Improvise] sign, which has already been discussed to some extent. As mentioned in Chap. 3, addressees are free to perform in any way and for however long they see fit when instructed to [Improvise] with no modifiers. However, if we consult the full definition of [Improvise] in Thompson's *Workbook 1*, it is clear that [Improvise] also emphasizes a particular relation between the addressee and the rest of the ensemble: "Perform a solo. This is the only sign in Soundpainting asking for an all-out solo to be performed. The Soloist has the freedom to fully go in any direction she/he chooses" (Thompson, 2006, p. 33). Calling for an "all-out solo," [Improvise] resembles the "improvised solo" of jazz music since the mid-twentieth century, implying a figure-ground-relation between the addressee's playing and that of the rest of the ensemble. Thompson's descriptions of the related what-signs [Background], "a repetitive, ostinato-like support behind a soloist" (Thompson, 2006, p. 30), and [Brush Work], "sparse support behind a soloist" (ibid., p. 31), reflect the idea of a soloist cast into the spotlight, performing on a background provided by other performers.

In my fieldwork, the [Improvise] sign has usually been addressed to one or two ensemble members at a time to yield an improvised solo and will be discussed here as such. But it would also be syntactically correct for the soundpainter to ask the whole ensemble to improvise: [Whole group]

[Improvise][Play] effectively corresponds to collective free improvisation, where all choices are left to performers. The figure/ground distinction usually implied by the [Improvise] sign obviously would not be as prevalent in that case. The rules mentioned in Chap. 3 about the termination of a solo that was initiated with [Improvise] would not apply in a situation of group improvisation like this.

Imbuing the performance of an ensemble member who is instructed to [Improvise] with a greater degree of solipsism than is implied by the notion of a "solo," the [Blinders] sign instructs ensemble members to "play their material without relating to each other, as if they were the only one in the room. In order to truly perform the [Blinders] sign, it is very important the performer does not relate with any other performer—no matter how close a performer's material is to another performer" (Thompson, 2010, p. 44). [Blinders] used in conjunction with [Improvise] sign (i.e., [Improvise][With][Blinders]) yields an improvised solo that avoids adapting to its immediate context, aiming to provide rich contrasts and unconventional, composite expressions across the ensemble (somewhat similarly to the effects of the [Play Can't Play] sign discussed above).

The many different ways of specifying and leaving open the relations between ensemble members can be combined, yielding many opportunities for social exchange, detachment, contrast, unity, etc., within the ensemble. Combining [Improvise][With][Blinders] and [Relate To], for instance, it is possible to sign [Brass 2][Improvise][With][Blinders][Slowly Enter], followed by [Brass 1][Relate To][Brass 2][Slowly Enter]. This would result in a situation where [Brass 2] is intentionally disregarding [Brass 1], but the opposite is true of [Brass 1], who is constantly aware of and relating to [Brass 2].

Consider the difference between [Brass 1][Brass 2][Improvise][With][Blinders][Slowly Enter] and [Brass 1][Brass 2][Relate To][Slowly Enter]: The former instruction lets individual ensemble members focus solely on their own ideas as they improvise, while the latter leads them to focus on the ideas of their peers. Or [Group 1][Minimalism][Play], followed by [Group 2][Relate To][Without][Minimalism][Play], which would yield both repetitive patterns from [Group 1] and related but non-repetitive musical utterances from [Group 2].

Superimposing, contrasting, and conjoining the contributions of ensemble members and subgroups in this way can lead to very interesting collective expressions. Using musician, composer, and improvisation scholar David Borgo's terms (2006), Soundpainting allows improvised interactions to achieve both "sync"- and "swarm"-like qualities. Participants may, as a result, learn a great deal about the possibility of peaceful coexistence between stark, musical contrasts. Or, conversely, they may begin to explore different modalities of musical cooperation and mutual attunement. Most importantly, these modes of interaction may be employed and substituted dynamically.

References

Becker, H. S. (1982). *Art Worlds*. University of California Press.
Belgrad, D. (2016). Improvisation, Democracy, and Feedback. In G. E. Lewis & B. Piekut (Eds.), *The Oxford Handbook of Critical Improvisation Studies* (Vol. 1, pp. 289–306). Oxford University Press.
Bertinetto, A. (2016). "Do not fear mistakes – there are none": The Mistake as Surprising Experience of Creativity in Jazz. In M. Santi & E. Zorzi (Eds.), *Education as Jazz: Interdisciplinary Sketches on a New Metaphor* (pp. 85–100). Cambridge Scholars Publishing.
Borgo, D. (2006). *Sync or Swarm: Improvising Music in a Complex Age*. Continuum Books.
Dempsey, N. P. (2008). Hook-Ups and Train Wrecks: Contextual Parameters and the Coordination of Jazz Interactions. *Symbolic Interaction, 31*(1), 57–75.
Duckert, K., & Rasmussen, G. (2013). *Sammenspil og improvisation med Soundpainting*. Edition Wilhelm Hansen.
Duckert, K., & Rasmussen, G. (2016). *Ensemble Playing and Improvisation with Soundpainting* (J. Faurholt, Ed.; S. Palmer, Trans.). Edition Wilhelm Hansen.
Faria, B. (2016). *Exercising Musicianship Anew Through Soundpainting: Speaking Music Through Sound Gestures*. Lund University.
Feisst, S. (2016). Negotiating Freedom and Control in Composition: Improvisation and Its Offshoots, 1950 to 1980. In G. Lewis & B. Piekut (Eds.), *The Oxford Handbook of Critical Improvisation Studies* (Vol. 2, pp. 206–229). Oxford University Press.
Fischlin, D., Heble, A., & Lipsitz, G. (2013). *The Fierce Urgency of Now: Improvisation, Rights, and the Ethics of Cocreation*. Duke University Press.
Kim, R. Y. (2012). John Cage in Separate Togetherness with Jazz. *Contemporary Music Review, 31*(1), 63–89.
Lewis, G. E. (1996). Improvised Music After 1950: Afrological and Eurological Perspectives. *Black Music Research Journal, 16*(1), 91–122.
Lewis, G. E. (2008). *A Power Stronger Than Itself: The AACM and American Experimental Music*. University of Chicago Press.
Luhmann, N. (2013). *Introduction to Systems Theory* (D. Baecker, Ed.; P. Gilgen, Trans.). Polity Press.

Martin, P. J. (2002). Spontaneity and Organisation. In D. Horn & M. Cooke (Eds.), *The Cambridge Companion to Jazz* (pp. 133–152). Cambridge University Press.

Minors, H. J. (2012). Reassessing the Thinking Body in Soundpainting. *How Performance Thinks*, 142–148.

Minors, H. J. (2020). Soundpainting: A Tool for Collaborating During Performance. In M. Blain & H. J. Minors (Eds.), *Artistic Research in Performance Through Collaboration* (pp. 113–138). Springer International Publishing. https://doi.org/10.1007/978-3-030-38599-6_7

Nyman, M. (1974). *Experimental Music: Cage and Beyond*. Studio Vista.

Piekut, B. (2011). *Experimentalism Otherwise: The New York Avant-Garde and Its Limits*. University of California Press.

Piekut, B. (2014). Indeterminacy, Free Improvisation, and the Mixed Avant-Garde: Experimental Music in London, 1965–1975. *Journal of the American Musicological Society, 67*(3), 769–823.

Thompson, W. (2006). *Soundpainting: The Art of Live Composition, Workbook 1*. Self-Published.

Thompson, W. (2010). *Soundpainting: The Art of Live Composition, Workbook 2*. Self-Published.

Thompson, W. (Director). (2017). *Soundpainting—Lesson 1—Walter Thompson* [Video recording]. YouTube. https://www.youtube.com/watch?v=YJQf0MDsNaA

Thompson, W., & Minors, H. J. (Directors). (2015a, January 18). *Soundpainting Interview with Walter Thompson Part 1* [Video]. YouTube. https://www.youtube.com/watch?v=oRLRVumJfhg

Thompson, W., & Minors, H. J. (Directors). (2015b, January 29). *Soundpainting Interview with Walter Thompson Part 3* [Video]. YouTube. https://www.youtube.com/watch?v=rzeuBP8BUxk

Thompson, W., & Minors, H. J. (Directors). (2015c, February 12). *Soundpainting Interview with Walter Thompson Part 4* [Video recording]. YouTube. https://www.youtube.com/watch?v=HWASsgNq1Rc

Toynbee, J. (2000). *Making Popular Music: Musicians, Creativity and Institutions*. Arnold.

Toynbee, J. (2012). Music, Culture, and Creativity. In M. Clayton, T. Herbert, & R. Middleton (Eds.), *The Cultural Study of Music: A Critical Introduction* (pp. 161–171). Routledge.

Vidal Belda, O. (2021). *Componiendo con soundpainting en el aula de música. Un estudio de casos colectivo sobre creación sonora colaborativa* (p. 1) [http://purl.org/dc/dcmitype/Text, Universitat de València]. https://dialnet.unirioja.es/servlet/tesis?codigo=301655

CHAPTER 5

Change, Freeze, Develop: Organization and Transformation

Most people are familiar with the situation where a brainstorming session has generated many different ideas. Being able to generate ideas and materials together is great. But what happens after the brainstorming? The generated ideas typically end up on a wall in the form of Post-it notes. In cases where a meeting participant snaps a photo in the hope of capturing the ideas for posterity, they may retain a digital afterlife. But the vast majority of such ideas probably never make it much further than that.

The transitory existence of those ideas may well be in line with the intentions of those who organized the meeting since the point of a brainstorm is to generate a plurality of ideas, not to solve a complex problem in one go. At other stages, for instance, in the process of designing a product, certain ideas may be selected, researched, elaborated, criticized, refined, and so on (Lerdahl, 2017). But in improvised music (and other improvised performance arts), the creative process is on display with an intrinsic, aesthetic value for the participants. In this context, it becomes necessary to move from generating a collection of musical ideas to selecting, refining, and organizing these ideas into a coherent, musical assemblage in the course of performance.

Whereas the examples of performative scenarios in the preceding chapters have been concerned with shorter segments of Soundpainting performances, this final chapter covers how Soundpainting provides ways of organizing the emerging content over the course of a whole performance.

© The Author(s), under exclusive license to Springer Nature Singapore Pte Ltd. 2024
A. Eskildsen, *Soundpainting*, Palgrave Studies in Sound,
https://doi.org/10.1007/978-981-96-1690-9_5

To produce coherence and interesting developments in longer segments of Soundpainting performances, Soundpainting provides a range of different methods for explicitly connecting to (or discarding) sounds produced by ensemble members in the immediate past, present, and future.

For Bruno Faria, a classically trained flutist, studying Soundpainting engendered a new way of thinking at a fundamental level about what a musician does, suggesting a distinction between "making the sound" and "making something with the sound" as distinct but overlapping intentionalities (Faria, 2016, p. 140). An important part of being a classical musician is being able to produce a sound as close to a prescribed ideal as possible, thus "making the sound." This could be replicated in Soundpainting using the [Palette] sign. But with open-content signs, there is no prescribed sound, and improvisation is required. Over time, Faria argues, having to respond to these signs leads performers to think musically in more holistic ways, to think about how musical gestures and sounds combine into larger assemblages, to think about "making something with the sound."

I am not from a classical background, but Faria's considerations resonate with me, as my own experience as a teacher of improvised music has shown how Soundpainting gives musicians who have little to no experience with improvisation a vocabulary with which to describe and understand different aspects of improvising. This is, however, not merely due to signs like [Scanning] or [Improvise] but also a consequence of how Soundpainting explicitly affords combining different musical voices and elements into larger pieces or creating content through direct dialogue and coaction.

This chapter begins by describing how Soundpainting deals with transitions between different sections in the performance. The chapter then proceeds to discuss how Soundpainting specifies its own internal time and prescribes different kinds of transformation of sonic content over time. The chapter argues that while the generation and distribution of sound and agency in Soundpainting performances rely upon the principles discussed in previous chapters, Soundpainting also provides unique means of organizing, sustaining, and transforming emergent, temporally extended patterns in the ongoing production of sound. As such, these possibilities for operation distinguish Soundpainting from other forms of improvisation while simultaneously highlighting how Soundpainting may be understood as a form of creativity akin to other kinds of experimental music, sound art, and human communication in general.

Connecting Actions

Some Soundpainting operations deal with the temporal form of a performance, both on an overall and a more immediate level, including the topic of transitions, which plays an important role in freer forms of improvised music as well. The soundpainter's instructions operate on a meta-level and can thus potentially refer to past, current, and future actions. Several signs provide ways for the interaction process to explicitly connect to (or disconnect from) actions taken by ensemble members.

A disconnect from present musical activities may occur, for instance, if different kinds of content are indicated in succession, as would be the case if [Whole Group][Long Tone][Play] were to be followed moments later by [Whole Group][Pointilism][Play], then moving on to [Whole Group][Minimalism][Play]. In this way, the performance jumps somewhat incoherently between different musical expressions with hard-edged, immediate transitions. Another example of a disconnective chain of events related not to musical content but to the social dimension would be if the phrase [Whole Group][Relate To][Play], which—as discussed in Chap. 4—instructs ensemble members to improvise with content that somehow relates to what others are doing, were to be followed by [Whole Group][Improvise][With][Blinders][Play], the exact opposite of the previous instruction, severing each ensemble member's connection to what others are doing.

Conversely, operations that connect to previous operations also occur in Soundpainting; instead of moving from one place to the next without looking back, the performance of some sort of content may be initiated and allowed to evolve gradually, for instance. This would be the case if the soundpainter were to sign [Whole Group][Relate To][Enter Slowly] and step back, letting the ensemble develop the emergent content on its own. Or, during or at the end of a performance, there might be a return to content performed at the beginning of the performance using the [Memory] sign (which will be discussed further below).

Soundpainters, ensemble members, audiences, or other observers may, of course, evaluate the sounding/performative result of these approaches to the large-scale form of a Soundpainting performance in different ways. Regardless of aesthetic inclinations, however, the interaction is always forced to perform selections regarding the connectivity between past, current, and future events. This is the case in any Soundpainting performance since even the simplest conceivable chain of events, such as a composition consisting only of [Whole Group][Long Tone][Play], must involve a termination of the performance using [Whole Group][Off] or a similar phrase to simply indicate a disconnect, a transition from activity to inactivity. Soundpainting thus involves a constant flux between (dis)connecting future events to current or past events. Crucially, this is not an optional aspect; the soundpainter (and thus the whole interaction system) is, with every single instruction phrase, forced to either connect to or disconnect from (parts of) the ongoing state of the performance at the time the phrase is signed.

Such connectivity is a general feature of communication, but since Soundpainting relies on a form of meta-communication to dynamically form musical connectivity, the tools for connecting actions across time are examined further below. A specific kind of connectivity, namely, transformation—from operations that entail immediate transformation to more gradual ones—is also discussed.

Past, Present, and Future

One of the simplest signs in Soundpainting is the [Continue] sign. In my encounters with Soundpainting practice, [Continue] has nonetheless constituted one of the most widely used and functionally important of all the Soundpainting signs. The instruction to [Continue] is aptly defined by Thompson in the following way: "Performer Continues with what she/he is performing" (Thompson, 2006, p. 38). Used for negation of discontinuity, i.e., in situations where ensemble members otherwise would not continue to do what they are doing, the [Continue] sign sustains the ongoing musical activity, entailing a direct continuity between the present and the immediate future.

Aside from supporting the ensemble's choices by indicating that they should indeed continue doing what they are doing (which can be necessary when working with beginners who do not yet understand that continuation during the soundpainter's signing of a new phrase is required), [Continue] is often used in conjunction with open signs that serve as both what- and when-signs, such as [Scanning] or [Point To Point]; if, for instance, during [Scanning], the soundpainter lets their arm rest above the head of a particular ensemble member and simultaneously signs [Continue], the ensemble member in question continues to play even after the soundpainter steps out of the box (usually, the ensemble member would stop performing at this point): "[Continue] may also be signed using just one hand in conjunction with another sign, such as [Point To Point] or [Scanning], indicating to the performer to [Continue] with the performed material after the Soundpainter removes the [Point] or the [Scan]" (Thompson, 2006, p. 38). [Continue] thus constitutes one of the most important editorial tools in Soundpainting, allowing the interaction system to not only generate different kinds of improvised content but also sustain and select among the content generated by ensemble members.

This is even more evident in a common strategy among soundpainters in which the whole ensemble is instructed to improvise; for instance, using a phrase like [Whole Group][Vamp][Play], the soundpainter listens to the result, draws a distinction within the generated content by signing [You (bass player)][You (singer)][Continue], [Rest of Group][Exit Slowly], and indicates which ensemble member actions are to be continued and which are to stop. The musical activity that remains can then be used for further operations, as in [Rest of Group][Synchronize][Enter Slowly], instructing the rest of the ensemble to copy what the bass player or the singer is doing, or [You (drummer)][Relate To][With][Vamp][Enter Slowly], instructing the drummer to perform something that relates to what the bass player and the singer are doing. Combining [Continue] with signs that draw distinctions among ensemble members ([You] and [Rest of Group] in this case, [Play Can't Play] could be another example) is one of the central ways in which Soundpainting explicitly discards some elements of musical communication (i.e., the actions taken by specific ensemble members) and connects to the remaining elements.

Related to [Continue], [Go Back To] instructs ensemble members to return to what they were instructed to do immediately before being instructed to do what they are currently doing. An example from Thompson's *Workbook 2* illustrates the use of [Go Back To]: "The group is performing a [Long Tone] and the Soundpainter signs [Whole Group] [Off], the group stops performing at the [Off] sign. The Soundpainter then signs [Go Back To][Slowly Enter]. The performers return to the previously performed [Long Tone] – playing the [Long Tone] exactly as is was played before signed [Off]" (Thompson, 2010, p. 34). While [Continue] connects the present moment with the immediate future, [Go Back To] connects the immediate future to the immediate past. [Continue] and [Go Back To] thus constitute two distinct recursive functions to organize the moment-to-moment flow of the performance.

Another related what-sign is the important [This], which simply refers to what the ensemble is doing in the present moment. Reminding us that Soundpainting is meta-communication, i.e., communication about the musical communication embodied in the musical sounds and actions taken by ensemble members, [This] is an example of self-observation where an interaction system operates directly on its constituent elements (i.e., the communicative actions of the interactants). While [This] in itself does not connect beyond the present moment in musical time but merely provides a way to refer to emergent musical content, said content is usually referred to in order to anticipate future content. When used in conjunction with the [Improvise] sign (yielding the composite what-sign [Improvise][With][This]), for instance, the musical content currently being performed becomes a constraint for the improvisation, a particular point of departure that the improviser is required to use in their solo. In this way, [This] entails reusing emergent content, connecting the present moment to the immediate future.

[This] is often used in conjunction with [Memory], another sign that entails an important recursive operation. [Whole Group][This (Is)][Memory 1] saves the current "state" of the interaction system in a memory slot, which can be recalled later on through the use of [Memory 1] as a what-sign. If the soundpainter signs [Whole Group][Minimalism][Play], the result will be a repeating set of simple, musical patterns, after which [Whole Group][This (Is)][Memory 1] (no when-sign is needed since no response from the ensemble is required) will instruct ensemble members to remember what/how they are performing in the present moment and be able to return to this state at a later point in time. [Whole Group][Memory 1][Play] is now a syntactically valid phrase. This gives the interaction system an explicitly mnemonic device, a recursive operation that allows for future use of emergent content even after other kinds of content have been performed. [This] and [Memory] are among Soundpainting's tools for generating musical form, explicitly indicating fixity by allowing for the recurrence and reuse of emergent content.

It should be noted that certain limitations pertain to the [Memory] gesture due to the limited short-term memory capacity of ensemble members. Even professional musicians may find it difficult to recall more than a couple of complex musical scenarios stored in short-term memory using the [Memory] gesture. Remembering one sustained note might be less difficult than remembering a complex groove, though, and one might speculate that the mileage of the ensemble's working memory varies according to the complexity of the material to be remembered.

Transformations

The final aspect of recursion to be discussed here is transformation, operations where the content being performed is fixed in some ways and transformed in other ways. The discussion progresses from signs that entail immediate transitions from one state or quality to another to signs that entail a more gradual process of transformation.

The simplest examples of operations that explicitly operate upon and transform content that is currently being performed are how-signs such as [Volume Fader], [Tempo Fader], and [More Space Fader], which specify a relative volume, tempo (which is relevant in cases where the performed content is organized by a musical meter), and "space" (which refers to the temporal density of the collective sound of the ensemble). The soundpainter's physical execution of these signs involves a kind of scale, in the form of either a vertical forearm on which the hand of the other arm can indicate a position or a virtual horizontal scale on which the soundpainter's hands can indicate relative positions. Syntactically, these how-signs can not only be used after a what-sign to specify aspects of future action to be taken (as in [Whole Group][Long Tone][Volume Fader (Low)][Play]) but can also act syntactically as a combined what- and when-sign which transforms the content currently being produced, as the use of [Whole Group][Pointilism][Play], followed by [Whole Group][More Space Fader], after which the soundpainter steps into the box and adjusts the [More Space Fader] to dynamically change the relative amount of space between sounds generated with [Pointilism]. These how-signs entail transformations along singular dimensions, while all other aspects remain fixed as they were before the transformation.

Aside from how-signs, several what-signs in Soundpainting involve operations that transform the content currently being performed on a broader scale than in the case of how-signs, which address a single parameter. Of this latter kind of transformation, the [Change] sign (which was mentioned briefly above in connection with [Point To Point]) and related signs such as [Change Add] and [Change Subtract] are perhaps the most obvious examples. Thompson defines [Change] in the following way: "The performer [Changes] her/his improvisation. The performer may choose something brand new or modify the material being performed" (Thompson, 2006, p. 28). If the phrase [Whole Group][Minimalism] [Play] has been used to initiate [Minimalism], the phrase [Whole Group] [Change][Play] instructs the ensemble to perform [Minimalism] again, this time with content that somehow differs from that which was previously played (other pitches, rhythms, style, etc.). When used in this way, [Change], requires the addressee to repeat the instruction but improvise new content. The frame remains fixed, but the content is generated anew.

Conversely, the related [Change Add] and [Change Subtract] signs transform the ongoing musical activity by "adding a small amount of new material to the existing material being performed" or instructing the addressee to "subtract a small part of the material you are playing and continue performing the remaining material" (Thompson, 2010, p. 61), respectively. In the context of [Minimalism], for instance, [Change Add] and [Change Subtract] could entail adding or removing a note in the recurring minimalist pattern, indicating a minor change.

Another immediate transformation of the musical content currently being performed is implied by the [Freeze] and [Stab Freeze] signs. [Freeze] entails "freezing material into a [Long Tone]" (Thompson, 2010, p. 33), and [Stab Freeze] instructs addressees to perform "a CD-like skip with the material being performed" (Thompson, 2006, p. 30). While [Freeze] operates at a granular level, [Stab Freeze] operates with a slightly longer yet still short timespan. Both signs entail zooming in on short samples of improvised or recurring content and reiterating them until the sign is terminated (or indefinitely, if the [Continue] sign is used). If the ensemble is performing a four-bar [Vamp], for instance, these signs can provide a radical transformation of the current content, potentially disrupting the established sense of metrically organized time. [Freeze] and [Stab Freeze] nonetheless indicate fixity; no transformation is expected to take place after content has been frozen. While the transformations discussed above generally occur at a certain point in time or over the course of a few seconds (indicated by when-signs such as [Play] and [Slowly Enter]), other signs entail a more gradual transformation.

In the cases of some of the open what-signs discussed at various points above, gradual transformation as the addressee is improvising is expected to occur according to three rules, which Thompson refers to as "rates of development":

1. [Point To Point] and [Scanning] are both gestures where the performer is required to develop their material at a slow rate. If you (the Soundpainter) have signed a player to [Continue], in [Point To Point] or [Scanning], the

performer develops their material in such a way that one minute later there would still be a relationship to their original idea.

2. With [Play Can't Play] and the [Develop] gesture, the rate of development is about twice as much as that of [Point To Point] or [Scanning] – a minute later there would only be a vague relationship to the original idea.

3. The Improvisation gesture is the only gesture in Soundpainting where the rate of development is left open to the performer – they can develop at any rate they desire. (Thompson, 2010, p. 6)

The open what-signs [Point To Point], [Scanning], [Play Can't Play], and [Improvise] (as well as [Develop], which will be discussed below) do not only indicate improvisation in terms of the content to be initiated according to the point of entry specified with the relevant when-sign but also entail a specified rate of improvisational development. To a certain extent, this is also true of the more fixed what-signs such as [Minimalism], [Vamp], [Melody], and [Long Tone]. In the former category (open signs), addressees are expected to develop the content in an improvised way, whereas this is not the case in the latter category (fixed signs).

The "development" of content required by these signs is open-ended, leaving the quality of the transformation open to performer choice, providing no endpoint, and specifying only a rough sense of the "rate" at which transformation should occur (c.f. the three rules mentioned above).

The what-sign [Morph], invented by the renowned bass player Mark Dresser, similarly entails a gradual transformation. Unlike the signs discussed above with regard to rates of development, which entail an open-ended process of development, [Morph] instructs addressees to perform "a slow progression from one Content to another" (Thompson, 2010, p. 37), syntactically requiring a combination with another what-sign which serves as the goal of the transformative operation.

Thompson refers to an example where the ensemble has been given the instruction [Whole Group][Long Tone][Play], and the soundpainter then signs [Whole Group][Morph][Pointillism][Slowly Enter]: "In this example the performer slowly introduces [Pointillism] just a little at a time and returns to the [Long Tone], progressively adding [Pointillism] a little more each time until only [Pointillism] is being performed" (ibid.). The duration of the transformation entailed by the [Morph] sign is 30 seconds by default but can be changed in rehearsal or by the soundpainter in the course of performance using the [Duration Fader] sign (ibid.). [Morph] thus clearly indicates fixity in terms of both the duration of the transformation, the starting point (i.e., [This]), and the endpoint (i.e., the what-sign with which [Morph] is juxtaposed). This implicitly leaves open the interpretation of how to transform one kind of content into another; instructions to [Morph] from [Minimalism] to [Speak] or from [Pointilism] to [Relate To], for instance, require addressees to draw their own distinctions regarding the ways in which one gradually moves between radically different kinds of content and/or social relation.

As a final analytical point, transformative operations can also involve improvisation, which develops somewhat organically based on the current musical situation. In a sense, this has already been discussed regarding the [Relate To] sign, and the possibilities of the [Relate To] sign will not be reiterated here. The composite what-sign [Improvise][With][This], however, similarly indicates an open-ended improvisation that is constrained at the outset by a requirement to use material similar to that which is currently being performed by the ensemble. Unlike [Relate To], [Improvise][With][This] does not require addressees to continually focus their attention on other ensemble members, only at first is the addressee expected to thoroughly listen to other ensemble members and imitate the content that they are performing.

As specified in Thompson's three aforementioned rules about "rate of development," however, [Improvise] entails that the "rate of development" is left open to performer choice, meaning that once the improvisation has begun, the addressee could very quickly develop the content into something very different. Furthermore, as discussed earlier, [Improvise] implies a soloistic role for the addressee. In cases where the total openness of [Improvise] is not deemed desirable, the [Develop] sign instructs addressees to "develop the material at a moderate pace" (Thompson, 2010, p. 44). If the soundpainter has signed [Whole Group][Long Tone][Play] and then signs [Whole Group][Develop][Slowly Enter], the ensemble will begin from a static set of sustained sounds and slowly begin to deviate from this, perhaps varying pitch, introducing rhythmicity, changing timbre, etc. [Develop] thus initiates an open-ended improvisation with a fixed starting point, namely, the content that is currently being performed.

Outcomes: Composition, Improvisation, and Beyond

Arriving at the conclusion of a Soundpainting session, we might wonder what the actual outcome or result is. What is constructed or achieved when Soundpainting is practiced? There is, of course, no universal answer to this question, as Soundpainting is used in diverse ways and different contexts.

One type of answer, however, involves what we can refer to as the production of a work of art—a composition created in the course of performance. To that end, long-time practitioners of Soundpainting may consider my construal of Soundpainting as a form of *conducted improvisation* somewhat inaccurate since Thompson defines Soundpainting as a "multidisciplinary live composing sign language" (Thompson, 2006, p. 5), preferring the terminology of "live composing" over "improvising." In Thompson's online instruction videos, however, the absence of pre-established scripts/scores and the importance of liveness and immediacy are emphasized as key aspects of Soundpainting:

> Soundpainting is communication with your group, you are composing in real time using a sign language. You have not given them notated music, choreography, or text for a play. It is done in real time, nothing is planned ahead of time, it is done in the moment. (Thompson, 2017, 13:45, my transcription)

By simultaneously arguing that Soundpainting performances are to be understood as compositions or "pieces," a position that denies any simple dichotomy between improvisation and composition is articulated. This position mirrors a broader development within the field of improvisation studies, where scholars argue that we need to understand the relationship between improvisation versus composition in more nuanced ways (Lewis & Piekut, 2016, p. 8).

Edgar Landgraf has discussed at length how Western cultural notions of improvisation and art have been deeply intertwined, at least since Romanticism, arguing that some of the expectations we hold for artworks apply in the context of improvisational performance as well. Like works of art, improvised performances are expected to generate interesting, inventive, artistic agency (Landgraf, 2011, p. 7). As this book has hopefully demonstrated, Soundpainting can be used to facilitate and generate improvisational, musical performance that exhibits inventiveness, etc. I thus generally agree with Thompson's discourse, i.e., that Soundpainting certainly can facilitate the creation of compositions as works of art—in the sense suggested by Landgraf.

But I would also like to open up the perspective to other significant outcomes; due to its interactive and improvised nature, Soundpainting engenders and relies upon what Ajay Heble and Daniel Fischlin have called an "ethics of co-creation" (Fischlin et al., 2013). The creative engine of Soundpainting relies upon a highly formalized yet very flexible system of communication and agency. Under the right circumstances, it supports and requires collaboration and commitment, generates possibilities and contexts for creative agency, and allows for contrasting and diverse musical forms of expression to coexist and interact productively.

Broader Perspectives

In the realm of musical practice, Soundpainting constitutes a unique and innovative approach. It is not merely a sign language for conducted improvisation but also a comprehensive system that fosters creativity, facilitates communication, and encourages collaboration. Soundpainting provides a structured yet flexible framework that allows for a wide and nuanced array of open-ended signs and content constraints. Moreover, Soundpainting addresses the challenge of organizing and transforming larger sections of improvised music into coherent pieces, enabling the creation of music that is not only improvised but also cohesive and meaningful. This dynamic interplay between structure and freedom is what sets Soundpainting apart and might serve as a practical model for further developments in constraint theory.

The syntax and general communication process in Soundpainting, with its meta-agentic focus, enhances the instructional capabilities of the sign language. It allows for the distribution of agency, both static and dynamic, thereby constructing relations among the participants. This aspect of Soundpainting is particularly noteworthy as it fosters a sense of shared responsibility and mutual respect among the performers. Scholars of creativity and collaboration should see this book and Soundpainting as a practice, as a source for insight into the collaborative, communicative, and interactive roots of creativity. As we continue to explore and understand Soundpainting, we can look forward to discovering new ways of making music and new insights into human creative processes.

References

Faria, B. (2016). *Exercising Musicianship Anew Through Soundpainting: Speaking Music Through Sound Gestures*. Lund University.

Fischlin, D., Heble, A., & Lipsitz, G. (2013). *The Fierce Urgency of Now: Improvisation, Rights, and the Ethics of Cocreation*. Duke University Press.

Landgraf, E. (2011). *Improvisation as Art: Conceptual Challenges, Historical Perspectives*. Continuum Books.

Lerdahl, E. (2017). *Nyskapning: Arbeidsbok i kreative metoder*. Gyldendal Akademisk.

Lewis, G. E., & Piekut, B. (2016). Introduction: On Critical Improvisation Studies. In G. E. Lewis & B. Piekut (Eds.), *The Oxford Handbook of Critical Improvisation Studies* (Vol. 1, pp. 1–37). Oxford University Press.

Thompson, W. (2006). *Soundpainting: The Art of Live Composition, Workbook 1*. Self-Published.

Thompson, W. (2010). *Soundpainting: The Art of Live Composition, Workbook 2*. Self-Published.

Thompson, W. (Director). (2017). *Soundpainting—Lesson 1—Walter Thompson* [Video recording]. YouTube. https://www.youtube.com/watch?v=YJQf0MDsNaA

The manufacturer's authorised representative in the EU is Springer Nature Customer Service Centre GmbH, Europaplatz 3, 69115 Heidelberg, Germany. If you have any concerns regarding our products, please contact ProductSafety@springernature.com

Printed and bound by CPI Group (UK) Ltd, Croydon, CR0 4YY
03/02/2026
02046976-0001